The Library of Greek Thought.

GREEK SOCIAL LIFE

EDITED BY
ERNEST BARKER, M.A., D.LITT., LL.D.
PRINCIPAL OF KING'S COLLEGE, UNIVERSITY OF LONDON

AMS PRESS
NEW YORK

GREEK
SOCIAL LIFE

BY

F. A. WRIGHT, M.A.

1925
LONDON & TORONTO
J. M. DENT & SONS LTD.
NEW YORK: E. P. DUTTON & CO.

Library of Congress Cataloging in Publication Data

Wright, Frederick Adam, 1869-1946, comp.
  Greek social life.

  Original ed. issued in series: The Library of
Greek thought.
    1. Greece--Social life and customs. 2. Greek
literature--Translations into English. 3. English
literature--Translation from Greek. I. Title.
II. Series: The Library of Greek thought.
DF78.A2W7 1973   913.38'03   70-179283
ISBN 0-404-07803-6

Reprinted from an original copy in the collections of
the Newark Public Library

Reprinted by arrangement with J.M. Dent & Sons Ltd.,
London, England

From the edition of 1925, London
First AMS edition published in 1973
Manufactured in the United States of America

AMS PRESS INC.
NEW YORK, N.Y. 10003

INTRODUCTION

IT might perhaps be possible to collect within the compass
of one small volume a series of passages, from Homer to
Agathias, which should illustrate the varying phases of
Greek social life in the Mediterranean countries during
fifteen centuries. But such a collection, though it would
have the fascination of a kaleidoscope, would also have its
bewildering inconsistencies; and on the whole it seems better,
considering the limitations of space, to confine our picture
chiefly to that period and that city which supplies us with
the largest amount of material, and only to consider here
with any fullness the conditions of society of Athens in the
fifth and fourth centuries B.C.

As a matter of fact, when we speak of Greek manners
we usually mean Athenian manners, even as when we speak
of Greek history we usually mean the period between the
Persian Wars and the death of Alexander. The very different
conditions that prevailed in Sparta are only taken into
account as a parenthesis, and the other states of Greece,
Corinth, Thebes, Argos, Thessaly and the rest, are almost
disregarded. Nor is this as unreasonable as it might seem.
Athens was the school of Greece, and her teaching extended
over all departments of life. When Athens rose to greatness,
Greece was great; when Athens fell, Greece shared in
her decline.

I have therefore discarded, I need not say how reluctantly,
most of the many passages in Homer that throw light upon
the social condition of early Greece; and have drawn very

sparingly on Hesiod, the gnomic and lyric poets, and the Ionians. For the same reason my quotations from Alexandrian literature and the Egyptian papyri, with all their wealth of intimate realism, have been severely restricted; and I have given scarcely more than a hint of the state of Greece under the Roman Empire. The process of elimination has been sufficiently painful; but it was necessary, if anything like an adequate picture of Athenian society was to be attempted.

The conditions under which the Athenians lived were so different from ours that they require and deserve careful study. But before descending to details it may be well to define as clearly as possible what an ancient Athenian meant, and what a modern Englishman means, by Society. An Englishman, when he is not at business or engaged in some form of outdoor sport, is normally to be found at home. His social duties and his social pleasures centre round his own hearth; and for social success his wife's personality is at least as important as his own. The Athenian on the other hand used his house chiefly as a place to sleep in, and of the many hours of his day only the smallest fraction was spent under the family roof. As for his wife, so far from sharing in her husband's recreations, she very rarely saw any man except her own near relatives, and lived a virtual prisoner within four walls. While with us most social functions are organised by women for women, in Attica it was exactly the reverse, they were organised there by men for men; and it is not altogether unjust to describe the Athens of the fifth century B.C. as "A small exclusive society of male slave owners, perfectly convinced of the inferiority of women, and thoroughly satisfied with themselves." In the following pages, therefore, the word "society" must be taken as meaning the society of men; women being regarded as but slightly superior to slaves, and both alike considered as created by nature for the gratification of the male.

II

It has been often said, and with truth, that Athens was
the most complete example of true democracy that the
world has ever seen. But this fact should not be held to
preclude the existence in the body politic of many different
classes, each with its own social rank. At the top of the
scale came the old families, the Eupatrids, whose origin in
many cases went back to the days of Solon and Pisistratus,
or even to the half-mythical time of Cecrops and Theseus.
For two centuries these families supplied the state with its
foremost soldiers and politicians, and if the number of
public offices that fell to their share appears somewhat
disproportionate, it should not be forgotten that even in a
democracy there is such a thing as inherited talent. Of one
such house, whose heads in alternate generations bore the
names of Dicaeogenes and Menexenus, we have a detailed
history in the Fifth Oration of Isaeus. There we see that
a Dicaeogenes was acting as general when killed in battle
at Eleusis, 457 B.C.; that his son led the cavalry at Spartolus,
429; and that his grandson, commanding a trireme, was
killed in a naval engagement at Cnidos, 411. This latter's
son is the object of some of Isaeus' choicest invective; but,
in spite of that, we know from inscriptions that his grandson,
another Dicaeogenes, was a member of the Board of Generals,
the chief executive of Athens, in the years 325 and 324 B.C.

This family may serve as a typical example of the semi-
official class, and there were many others of the same
position; those, for example, to which belonged Miltiades
and his son Cimon, Melesias and his son Thucydides,
Hipponicus and his son Callias; most famous of all perhaps
for the ability of its members, though suffering from something of the same stigma of doubtful reputation as did the
Claudians at Rome, the great clan of the Alcmaeonidae.

Its record begins in ancient Athens with the Alcmaeon
who was responsible for the sacrilegious murder of Cylon,
incurring thereby a taint from which his descendants never
quite escaped. His son Megacles, as leader of the aristocrats,
spent a long life in alternate quarrels and reconciliations
with the tyrant Pisistratus, to whom he married his daughter.
The second Alcmaeon, grandson of the first, was a friend
of King Croesus, and established the family fortune in the
manner described by Herodotus, his wealth being further
increased in the next generation by the marriage of his son,
the second Megacles, to Agarista, daughter of the tyrant
of Sicyon. The offspring of this union was Clisthenes, the
greatest of Athenian statesmen, called after his maternal
grandfather; and by their mothers, a second Agarista and
Dinomache, Pericles and Alcibiades were both members
of the clan.

Most of these great houses so far resembled our ducal
families that their revenues came chiefly from the possession
of land and house property; and by Athenian standards,
some of them were very wealthy. The yearly income of the
second Dicaeogenes is estimated by Isaeus as amounting
to eighty minae, in English money about three hundred
pounds; which, with the purchasing value of money about
twelve times greater than ours, was reckoned, under Athenian
conditions, quite a handsome fortune. Their chief rivals,
both in material riches and in social importance, came from
the next class, that of the big manufacturers, possessors
sometimes of thousands of slaves who took the place of
machinery and were their masters' living tools. Such a one
was Nicias, commander of the ill-fated Sicilian expedition
and the most universally respected man of his time, who,
besides owning smaller factories, had over a thousand slaves
working for him in the silver mines at Laurium. Another
rich manufacturer was Demosthenes, father of the great

orator, who directed at least two important businesses, and left his son an inheritance of fifteen talents, roughly speaking nearly four thousand pounds. A third—although in this case he was not an Athenian citizen but a resident alien—was Cephalus, father of the orator Lysias, whose portrait is so charmingly drawn by Plato in the opening pages of the *Republic*. We do not know the amount of Cephalus' own fortune, except that it was less than his grandfather and larger than his father had left behind them, but we have some figures for the family property in the next generation. When the Thirty Tyrants fell short of money, they made a list of ten resident aliens whose goods might be conveniently confiscated. On that list were the names of Lysias and his brother Polemarchus, and we know from the orator's own statements that they then had three houses expensively furnished, a factory with a stock in hand of seven hundred shields, one hundred and twenty skilled slave workmen, and in one chest a sum of money amounting in our coinage to about a thousand pounds.

Only a little way behind the landed proprietors and the manufacturers in the matter of accumulated wealth came the bankers and money-lenders of the Piraeus; but as they were mostly resident aliens of foreign extraction, their social influence was comparatively slight. At the other end of the money scale came the crowd of seafaring folk—fishers, longshoremen and mariners—who thronged the streets and docks around the harbour, or lived scattered in little hamlets along the coast of Attica. But the very large majority of the twenty thousand Athenian citizens, those who gave the city its particular tone and character, were neither rich nor poor. They were essentially middle class, the backbone of a democratic state, equally suspicious of the oligarchic noble and the ambitious demagogue. The farmers, who lived in the country and were only driven into town by stress of war, can hardly have affected the life of the city very greatly. But many of the habitual town dwellers owned minute estates—an acre or two of olive trees, a few patches of corn and green-stuff, some beehives and a tiny orchard—which they cultivated from the city, paying an occasional visit, like Lysias' client Euphiletos, when not otherwise occupied; and at other times apparently leaving them to the care of a slave or hired labourer. Others were the proprietors of shops, sellers of lamps like the famous demagogue Hyperbolus, greengrocers like Euripides' mother, barbers, confectioners, innkeepers, perfumers. Others again, like the tanner Cleon, followed a trade or profession, and were potters, masons, shoemakers, painters, doctors, sculptors. And all alike, until they were sixty, might be called upon, and usually were called upon, to leave their homes for several months in the year and serve in the army or on board the fleet. It was not till after his sixth decade that the true democrat really entered into his own; becoming then eligible for an old-age pension, and earning that pension by the performance of what was to him the most enjoyable of all duties, sitting day by day as juryman in the public law courts.

III

The Heliaea served as a convenient meeting-place for all the elderly citizens, and an Athenian dicast was as much attached to his own particular court as a retired colonel with us is to his own particular club. Any Athenian who liked and had nothing better to do could be always sure of a day's enjoyment and a day's employment in the jury courts. Every juryman had the satisfaction of knowing that for the moment he was an all-powerful arbiter, and the fivepenny fee, modest though it seems to us, was just about adequate for a day's subsistence. To the courts came cases from many over-sea states, and moreover before them every executive officer had to give an account of his year's work, so that they were, in fact, the centre cogwheel of the whole political and social system.

The law courts accordingly were much more popular with the ordinary citizen than was the Assembly, where attendance was unpaid and most of the business had been arranged beforehand by a committee of the Council, leaving nothing for the people to do but to say yes or no. At a national crisis, or when some great speaker was expected to make a special effort, the Pnyx would be crowded; but on many days something like methods of gentle compulsion were necessary to draw an audience from the Agora.

In the Agora itself there was no need to collect a crowd, for here was the great rendezvous for everyone in Athens, slave or free, citizen or foreigner. All through the forenoon the market district, with its temples and fountains, its statues and colonnades, would be thronged with buyers and sellers of fruit and eggs, bread, oil and wine. From the country districts outside the walls little droves of pigs and goats would arrive, driven in for sacrifice; from the Piraeus loads of fish just fresh from the sea. And those who had nothing to buy or sell came to see and be seen, to glance at the latest pottery ware, to turn the pages of the newest treatise of Anaxagoras, and above all to learn the news of the day, which, if it were not invented in the barbers' shops about the Agora, at least from them was most readily spread abroad.

In law court, assembly and market the reason that ostensibly brought men together was business. But the Athenian was a gregarious creature, and when the common work was done he usually joined with his fellows in common recreation. It is true that Athens had nothing very closely corresponding to the great gatherings of a London season—Ascot and Goodwood, Wimbledon and Henley, Hurlingham and Lord's. The nearest equivalent to these in Athens were the great religious festivals, such as the Panathenaea and the Dionysia; in outside Greece the athletic competitions, such as the Olympic Games. But to the Athenians Olympia never made a very strong appeal: Elis was a long way from Attica, and a true Athenian, like a true Parisian, was never quite comfortable outside his beloved city.

In the place of these competitive athletics the Athenian substituted physical exercises carried on in gymnasia and palaestrae. On the running track and in the wrestling school he usually spent some hours each day, and about them centred a considerable portion of his social life. His day, indeed, would normally consist of some such a round as this: an early breakfast followed by a walk and talk with a friend, then attendance at the market or assembly, or on special occasions at a temple sacrifice, followed usually by another walk and another talk; then a light lunch and a siesta before going to the gymnasium. A careful oiling of the body before exercise, a spell of wrestling and gymnastics, a cold bath and elaborate massage occupied the afternoon; and in the evening a stroll and light conversation passed the time until the hour came for that convivial entertainment which in Greek is called a "symposium."

A symposium was so essentially an Athenian institution that it deserves description. The word itself would imply a drinking-party, and the inference is so far correct that eating played a very small part in the entertainment. There was a good deal of drinking—wine copiously diluted with water—and those whose heads were not too strong often found themselves overcome. But the chief form of amusement was once again—talk. As a slight change from conversation there might be a song or two, a patriotic ballad like the *Harmodius* :

I'll wreathe my sword with myrtle bough,
The sword that laid the tyrant low;—

or an impromptu catch started by one guest and capped by the others in turn. The invention of Limericks also was a favourite diversion, and Aristophanes at the end of *The Wasps* gives half a dozen specimens. Here is one of them:

> An amateur, driving too fast,
> From his car to the roadway was cast;
> And a friend kindly said, as he bandaged his head—
> "Mr. Cobbler, stick to your last."

Jocular comparisons, riddles, simple games, such as "Kottabos," and an occasional flute-girl or juggler served as other interludes to the main business of the evening, which went on pretty steadily; and if the company were sufficiently fond of the sound of their own voices, a symposium was quite capable of lasting till daybreak.

IV

It may be well at this point to follow Pericles' example and say a few words about women, remembering always that statesman's own dictum—"That woman is best who is least spoken of among men, whether for good or for evil." Women at Athens may be divided roughly into six categories. The first was composed of the free-born Athenians, the offspring of a formally contracted marriage between an Athenian man and woman, and themselves the sole possible wives allowed to an Athenian citizen. They, indeed, were the only women who had any legal rights whatever, and those rights were of the most severely restricted nature. Their marriages and divorces were arranged for them by their male relatives; they could not in their own persons inherit property, but were regarded as an appanage of the estate; even in the case of the children, whom they bore at the risk of their lives, the husband was absolute master, and could refuse existence to any infant that he himself did not desire. Their education was trivial, they were married very young, and they spent most of their days indoors, an occasional religious feast or family ceremonial being their only chance of free intercourse with the outer world. For social purposes they were by the Athenians, and may here by us, be regarded as perfectly negligible.

The next category, the " hetairai," lived in Athens, but were not of Athens. They were free foreign women who, relying on their personal attractions, had come to the city, or, more often probably, had been invited there by some travelled citizen under whose protection they were domiciled. A great deal has been written about these ladies, both in ancient and modern times; Athenaeus devotes a large part of the Thirteenth Book of the *Deipnosophistae* to them, and some recent authors have likened their influence in Greece to that which was exercised by women in France at the courts of Louis XIV. and Louis XV. But at Athens, throughout the fifth century B.C. and during the first half, at least, of the fourth century, their numbers and their social importance must have been small. The whole trend of Athenian literature shows that in that period comparatively few men took any pleasure in women's society; and of those few not many could have been able to afford the expense of a " female friend." The Hellenistic Age was when the great hetairai flourished—Thaïs, Glycera, Leontium, Gnathaena, Phryne and the rest—for women then, released from their Attic seclusion, began to play an equal part with men in affairs, and the riches of Asia, flowing into Greek pockets, made every sort of luxury possible.

As for the remaining four classes of women, little here need be said, since, being all slaves, they were not supposed to have feelings and cannot therefore be considered in the light of social creatures. The most useful were the maidservants, who at Athens were very numerous and could

either be hired for a fixed period or bought in perpetual
ownership. The poorest household usually possessed one
maid, but often only one; and in that case, as we see in the
speech of Lysias, *De caede Eratosthenis*, it fell to her lot
to clean the house, prepare the meals, see to the children,
and do the family marketing. More ornamental, but less
actually necessary, were the flute-girls and singers, the
female jugglers and acrobats, whose business it was to fill
up the gaps of conversation and enliven the proceedings at
a men's dinner party. They were normally not resident at
Athens, but, as the property of some foreign impresario,
moved about from city to city in Greece wherever it was
thought that men needed entertainment. To men's welfare
also the "pallakai," or private concubines, ministered; for
when a wife ceased to be physically attractive, if an Athenian
could afford the expense, a concubine was thought desirable
in the interests of health. Occasionally—the Athenians
were always economical—two men would share one concubine between them, and when she ceased to please she
could always be sold again; usually to fall into the lowest
class of all, and become an inmate of one of those closed
brothels which Solon first had legalised.

V

If we attempt now to sum up the good and bad points of
Athenian life, we shall find something like this. On the one
hand a keen sense of civic duty, a refined artistic taste, a
genuine moderation in all matters of eating and drinking,
a love of knowledge that lasted till death, and an insistence
on physical fitness as one of the duties of life. In the words
of Pericles, Athens "combined economy with culture, and
was refined without being effeminate." Curiously enough,
our chief national vices were precisely those for which the

xviGREEK SOCIAL LIFE

Athenians had little inclination. Intemperance, snobbishness, ostentation, hypocrisy doubtless existed to some degree among them; but they never reached the heights to which we have attained, and the gruesome figure of Mrs. Grundy would have seemed at Athens merely absurd. So much for the credit account. On the other side we see a coarseness, amounting often to actual indecency, in all matters of sexual conduct, and a toleration of unnatural vice; a very low standard of honesty and veracity, which rendered an Athenian politician particularly open to bribes and an Athenian merchant particularly inclined to sharp practices; worst of all, a profound and inveterate selfishness, which blinded men to the intolerable wrongs that every day they inflicted on their women and their slaves. Their level of intellect and taste was very high; their level of morals and humanity low.

In art and in literature they are still our masters, and when we diverge from the standards they have set up for us there, we do so at our own risk, and generally to our own hurt. But in the sphere of social life the case is different; and a study of the passages contained in this volume will probably show at least as many things to avoid as to imitate.

Messrs. Routledge have kindly allowed me the use of their edition of Frere's *Aristophanes*, and I have to thank Messrs. Macmillan for permission to quote from Mr. Dakyns' translation of Xenophon's *Oeconomicus*. In the Homer I have followed Derby and Cowper, in the Herodotus Cary; the other versions in this volume are my own attempts.

CONTENTS

THE HOMERIC AGE

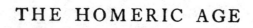

THE HOMERIC AGE

The City at Peace and War

HOMER, *Iliad* xviii. 490–606.

The *Iliad* lends itself less than the *Odyssey* to the portrayal of social customs, but in the scenes depicted on the shield of Achilles we have an unique picture of the everyday life of the Mycenaean Age.

AND two fair populous towns were sculptur'd there:
In one were marriage pomp and revelry,
And brides, in gay procession, through the streets
With blazing torches from their chambers borne,
While frequent rose the hymeneal song.
Youths whirl'd around in joyous dance, with sound
Of flute and harp; and, standing at their doors,
Admiring women on the pageant gaz'd.
Meanwhile a busy throng the forum fill'd:
There between two a fierce contention rose,
About a death-fine; to the public one
Appeal'd, asserting to have paid the whole;
While one denied that he had aught receiv'd.
Both were desirous that before the Judge
The issue should be tried; with noisy shouts
Their sev'ral partisans encourag'd each.
The heralds still'd the tumult of the crowd:
On polish'd chairs, in solemn circle, sat
The rev'rend Elders; in their hands they held
The loud-voic'd heralds' sceptres; waving these,
They heard th' alternate pleadings; in the midst
Two talents lay of gold, which he should take
Who should before them prove his righteous cause.

Before the second town two armies lay,
In arms refulgent; to destroy the town
Th' assailants threaten'd, or among themselves
Of all the wealth within the city stor'd
An equal half, as ransom, to divide.
The terms rejecting, the defenders mann'd
A secret ambush; on the walls they plac'd
Women and children muster'd for defence,
And men by age enfeebled; forth they went,
By Mars and Pallas led; these, wrought in gold,
In golden arms array'd, above the crowd
For beauty and stature, as befitting Gods,
Conspicuous shone; of lesser height the rest.
But when the destin'd ambuscade was reach'd,
Beside the river, where the shepherds drove
Their flocks and herds to water, down they lay,
In glitt'ring arms accoutred; and apart
They plac'd two spies, to notify betimes
Th' approach of flocks of sheep and lowing herds.
These, in two shepherds' charge, ere long appear'd,
Who, unsuspecting as they mov'd along,
Enjoy'd the music of their past'ral pipes.
They on the booty, from afar discern'd,
Sprang from their ambuscade; and cutting off
The herds, and fleecy flocks, their guardians slew.
Their comrades heard the tumult, where they sat
Before their sacred altars, and forthwith
Sprang on their cars, and with fast-stepping steeds
Pursued the plund'rers, and o'ertook them soon.
There on the river's bank they met in arms,
And each at other hurl'd their brazen spears.
And there were figur'd Strife, and Tumult wild,
And deadly Fate, who in her iron grasp
One newly-wounded, one unwounded bore,

While by the feet from out the press she dragg'd
Another slain: about her shoulders hung
A garment crimson'd with the blood of men.
Like living men they seem'd to move, to fight,
To drag away the bodies of the slain.

And there was grav'n a wide-extended plain
Of fallow land, rich, fertile, mellow soil,
Thrice plough'd; where many ploughmen up and down
Their teams were driving; and as each attain'd
The limit of the field, would one advance,
And tender him a cup of gen'rous wine:
Then would he turn, and to the end again
Along the furrow cheerly drive his plough.
And still behind them darker show'd the soil,
The true presentment of a new-plough'd field,
Though wrought in gold; a miracle of art.

There too was grav'n a corn-field, rich in grain,
Where with sharp sickles reapers plied their task;
The binders, following close, the bundles tied:
Three were the binders; and behind them boys
In close attendance waiting, in their arms
Gather'd the bundles, and in order pil'd.
Amid them, staff in hand, in silence stood
The King, rejoicing in the plenteous swathe.
A little way remov'd, the heralds slew
A sturdy ox, and now beneath an oak
Prepar'd the feast; while women mix'd, hard by,
White barley porridge for the lab'rers' meal.

And, with rich clusters laden, there was grav'n
A vineyard fair, all gold; of glossy black
The bunches were, on silver poles sustain'd;
Around, a darksome trench; beyond, a fence
Was wrought, of shining tin; and through it led
One only path, by which the bearers pass'd,

Who gather'd in the vineyard's bounteous store.
There maids and youths, in joyous spirits bright,
In woven baskets bore the luscious fruit.
A boy, amid them, from a clear-ton'd harp
Drew lovely music; well his liquid voice
The strings accompanied; they all with dance
And song harmonious join'd, and joyous shouts,
As the gay bevy lightly tripp'd along.

Of straight-horn'd cattle too a herd was grav'n;
Of gold and tin the heifers all were wrought:
They to the pasture, from the cattle-yard,
With gentle lowings, by a babbling stream,
Where quiv'ring reed-beds rustled, slowly mov'd.
Four golden shepherds walk'd beside the herd,
By nine swift dogs attended; then amid
The foremost heifers sprang two lions fierce
Upon the lordly bull: he, bellowing loud,
Was dragg'd along, by dogs and youths pursued.
The tough bull's-hide they tore, and gorging lapp'd
Th' intestines and dark blood; with vain attempt
The herdsmen following closely, to th' attack
Cheer'd their swift dogs; these shunn'd the lions' jaws.
And close around them baying, held aloof.

And there the skilful artist's hand had trac'd
A pasture broad, with fleecy flocks o'erspread,
In a fair glade, with fold, and tents, and pens.

There, too, the skilful artist's hand had wrought,
With curious workmanship, a mazy dance,
Like that which Daedalus in Cnossus erst
At fair-hair'd Ariadne's bidding fram'd.
There, laying each on other's wrists their hand,
Bright youths and many-suitor'd maidens danc'd:
In fair white linen these; in tunics those,
Well woven, shining soft with fragrant oils;

These with fair coronets were crown'd, while those
With golden swords from silver belts were girt.
Now whirl'd they round with nimble practis'd feet,
Easy, as when a potter, seated, turns
A wheel, new fashion'd by his skilful hand,
And spins it round, to prove if true it run:
Now featly mov'd in well-beseeming ranks.
A num'rous crowd, around, the lovely dance
Survey'd, delighted; while with measur'd chant
Two tumblers, in the midst, were whirling round.

DERBY.

Nausicaa

HOMER, *Odyssey* vi. 48–161.

The *Odyssey* is full of vivid descriptions of households, the dwellings of Circe and Calypso, the palaces of Menelaus and Alcinous, and the home of Odysseus himself. But the most intimate of all these passages are those in which Nausicaa appears.

Now came Aurora bright-enthroned, whose rays
Awaken'd fair Nausicaa; she her dream
Remember'd wond'ring, and her parents sought
Anxious to tell them. Them she found within.
Beside the hearth her royal mother sat,
Spinning soft fleeces with sea-purple dyed
Among her menial maidens, but she met
Her father, whom the Nobles of the land
Had summon'd, issuing abroad to join
The illustrious Chiefs in council. At his side
She stood, and thus her filial suit preferr'd.
    Sir! wilt thou lend me of the royal wains
A sumpter-carriage? for I wish to bear
My costly cloaths, but sullied and unfit
For use, at present, to the river side.
It is but seemly that thou should'st repair

Thyself to consultation with the Chiefs
Of all Phaeacia, clad in pure attire;
And my own brothers five, who dwell at home,
Two wedded, and the rest of age to wed,
Are all desirous, when they dance, to wear
Raiment new bleach'd; all which is my concern.
  So spake Nausicaa; for she dared not name
Her own glad nuptials to her father's ear,
Who, conscious yet of all her drift, replied.
  I grudge thee neither mules, my child, nor aught
That thou canst ask beside. Go, and my train
Shall furnish thee a sumpter-carriage forth
High-built, strong-wheel'd, and of capacious size.
  So saying, he issued his command, whom quick
His grooms obey'd. They in the court prepared
The sumpter-carriage, and adjoin'd the mules.
And now the virgin from her chamber, charged
With raiment, came, which on the car she placed,
And in the carriage-chest, meantime, the Queen,
Her mother, viands of all kinds disposed,
And fill'd a skin with wine. Nausicaa rose
Into her seat; but, ere she went, received
A golden cruse of oil from the Queen's hand
For unction of herself, and of her maids.
Then, seizing scourge and reins, she lash'd the mules.
They trampled loud the soil, straining to draw
Herself with all her vesture; nor alone
She went, but follow'd by her virgin train.
At the delightful rivulet arrived
Where those perennial cisterns were prepared
With purest crystal of the fountain fed
Profuse, sufficient for the deepest stains,
Loosing the mules, they drove them forth to browse
On the sweet herb beside the dimpled flood.

The carriage, next, light'ning, they bore in hand
The garments down to the unsullied wave,
And thrust them heap'd into the pools, their task
Dispatching brisk, and with an emulous haste.
When they had all purified, and no spot
Could now be seen, or blemish more, they spread
The raiment orderly along the beach
Where dashing tides had cleansed the pebbles most,
And laving, next, and smoothing o'er with oil
Their limbs, all seated on the river's bank,
They took repast, leaving the garments, stretch'd
In noonday fervour of the sun, to dry.
Their hunger satisfied, at once arose
The mistress and her train, and putting off
Their head-attire, play'd wanton with the ball,
The Princess singing to her maids the while.
Such as shaft-arm'd Diana roams the hills,
Täygetus sky-capt, or Erymanth,
The wild boar chasing, or fleet-footed hind,
All joy; the rural nymphs, daughters of Jove,
Sport with her, and Latona's heart exults;
She high her graceful head above the rest
And features lifts divine, though all be fair,
With ease distinguishable from them all;
So all her train she, virgin pure, surpass'd.

But when the hour of her departure thence
Approach'd (the mules now yoked again, and all
Her elegant apparel folded neat),
Minerva azure-eyed mused how to wake
Ulysses, that he might behold the fair
Virgin, his destin'd guide into the town.
The Princess, then, casting the ball toward
A maiden of her train, erroneous threw
And plunged it deep into the dimpling stream.

All shrieked; Ulysses at the sound awoke,
And, sitting, meditated thus the cause.
　　Ah me! what mortal race inhabit here?
Rude are they, contumacious and unjust?
Or hospitable, and who fear the Gods?
So shrill the cry and feminine of nymphs
Fills all the air around, such as frequent
The hills, clear fountains, and herbaceous meads.
Is this a neighbourhood of men endued
With voice articulate? But what avails
To ask; I will myself go forth and see.
　　So saying, divine Ulysses from beneath
His thicket crept, and from the leafy wood
A spreading branch pluck'd forcibly, design'd
A decent screen effectual, held before.
So forth he went, as goes the lion forth,
The mountain-lion, conscious of his strength,
Whom winds have vex'd and rains; fire fills his eyes,
And whether herds or flocks, or woodland deer
He find, he rends them, and, athirst for blood,
Abstains not even from the guarded fold,
Such sure to seem in virgin eyes, the Chief,
All naked as he was, left his retreat,
Reluctant, by necessity constrain'd.
Him foul with sea foam horror-struck they view'd,
And o'er the jutting shores fled all dispersed.
Nausicaa alone fled not; for her
Pallas courageous made, and from her limbs,
By pow'r divine, all tremor took away.
Firm she expected him; he doubtful stood,
Or to implore the lovely maid, her knees
Embracing, or aloof standing, to ask
In gentle terms discreet the gift of cloaths,
And guidance to the city where she dwelt.

Him so deliberating, most, at length,
This counsel pleas'd; in suppliant terms aloof
To sue to her, lest if he clasp'd her knees,
The virgin should that bolder course resent.
Then gentle, thus, and well-advised he spake.
    Oh, Queen! thy earnest suppliant I approach.
Art thou some Goddess, or of mortal race?
For if some Goddess, and from heaven arrived,
Diana, then, daughter of mighty Jove
I deem thee most, for such as hers appear
Thy form, thy stature, and thy air divine.
But if, of mortal race, thou dwell below,
Thrice happy then, thy parents I account,
And happy thrice thy brethren. Ah! the joy
Which always for thy sake their bosoms fill,
When thee they view, all lovely as thou art,
Ent'ring majestic on the graceful dance.
But him beyond all others blest I deem,
The youth, who, wealthier than his rich compeers,
Shall win and lead thee to his honour'd home.
For never with these eyes a mortal form
Beheld I comparable aught to thine,
In man or woman. Wonder-wrapt I gaze.
COWPER.

EARLY GREECE AND IONIA

EARLY GREECE AND IONIA

The Creation of Woman

HESIOD, *Works and Days* 59–89.

The gift of female society to man is described by Hesiod in an even more pessimistic spirit than that which inspires the Jewish narrative. For Hesiod, woman is not a doubtful blessing but a definite curse, and her creation by God is not an act of benevolence but a punishment.

AND the father of men and gods bade famous Hephaestus to hasten and mix earth with water, and to put therein mortal speech and strength, and to fashion a fair maiden's shape, lovely and like to the immortal goddesses in visage. Athene was to teach her handiwork and the weaving of the bright web, and golden Aphrodite was to shed grace upon her head and grievous desire and wasting care. And he ordered Hermes, the swift slayer of Argus, to set within her a dog's shameless mind and thievish ways.

So he spake. And they obeyed King Zeus, the son of Cronos. The famous Limper moulded clay forthwith into the semblance of a modest maid, even as the son of Cronos willed. The goddess bright-eyed Athene gave her a girdle and scented robes; the divine Graces and queen Persuasion put upon her neck golden chains; and the fair-tressed Hours wreathed her head with spring flowers. Within her breast also the swift slayer of Argus, the herald of the gods, fashioned lies and crafty words and thievish ways. And he called this woman Pandora, because all the dwellers on Olympus had given a gift to be a plague to men who eat bread.

And when he had completed the sheer hopeless snare the

Father sent the famous slayer of Argus, the swift messenger
of the gods, to take it, as a gift, to Epimetheus. Nor did
Epimetheus bethink him of how Prometheus had said:
"Take not ever a gift from Olympian Zeus. Send it back
to him rather, lest it prove something deadly to men."
He took that gift, and when he had the evil thing, then
he understood.

Rules of Conduct

HESIOD, *Works and Days* (a) 302–319, (b) 405–413, (c) 695–705.

(a) The Law of Work.

Hunger, look you, is a meet reward for the man who will
not work. Gods and men are angry with the sluggard, for
he is like in temper to the stingless drones who spoil the
labours of the bees, eating without working. Love your
land and keep it in good trim, so that your barns may be full
of provision in due season. From well-worked fields men
grow rich in flocks and substance, and labour renders them
dearer to the immortal gods. Work is no disgrace; it is a
disgrace to be idle. If you work, the sluggard will soon
envy your riches, for merit and renown attend on wealth.
Whatever be your fortune, work is best; if you will turn
your foolish thoughts away from other men's possessions
to your own task, and think of getting a livelihood, as I
bid you. It is the evil kind of shame that attends the needy
man; for shame is both a curse and a blessing to mortals.
Shame goes with poverty, boldness with wealth.

(b) The Needs of Life.

First get a house, and a woman, and an ox for the plough
—a slave woman, not a wife, to follow the oxen—and then
get for yourself all the gear that is wanted in a house, so that
you may not have to ask of another, and he refuse, and you

be without while the season is passing, and your field is spoiling. Never defer a thing till to-morrow or the day after. A poor worker never fills his barn nor yet one who puts work off. Care makes work prosper: but a man who puts off things is always wrestling with ruin.

(c) *The Marriage Age.*

Bring home a wife to your house when you are ripe for marriage, not far short of thirty years nor much above: that is the right season for wedlock. Let your wife have been four years a woman, and marry her in the fifth. Marry a maiden, so that you can teach her good ways, and marry for preference some one who lives near you—after you have looked about you well, lest your marriage be a joke for your neighbours. There is nothing a man can win which is better than a good wife; and there is nothing worse than a bad wife, a greedy woman who singes her man without fire, strong though he be, and brings him to old age before his time.

Winter Miseries

HESIOD, *Works and Days* 504–535.

Beware of the mid-winter month, Lenaeon, with its evil days, fit to skin an ox, and its cruel frosts which fall upon the earth when the north wind blows. Across horse-breeding Thrace he blows upon the broad sea and stirs up the waves; and the earth and the woodland roars. Many a high oak and sturdy pine he brings down to bounteous earth beneath his onrush in the mountain glens, and all the wide forest shrieks aloud, and the beasts shiver and tuck their tails under their legs, even those that have fur to protect their skin: for so cold is he that he blows even through them, although they are shaggy of breast. He gets through an ox hide; it cannot stop him. He blows even through a goat's long hair. But through the fleeces of sheep the strength of the north wind cannot blow; their wool is too abundant. He makes the old man bend like a wheel; but he does not plow through the soft-skinned maid who stays within doors by her dear mother's side, knowing naught as yet of golden Aphrodite's works, and washes well her tender body, and anoints herself with oil, and lies in a close room within the house, on a winter's day when Old Boneless gnaws his foot in the wretched place that is his fireless home; for the sun shows him no pasture whither he may go, but turns in heaven over the folk and city of swarthy men and gives but little light to all the peoples of Hellas. Then the creatures of the wood, horned and unhorned alike, their teeth miserably chattering, flee through the wooded glades, and in their minds all have but one thought, to seek shelter and find some close covert or rocky cave. Then like the Three-legged One, whose back is broken and his head looks down to earth, like him they wander, trying to escape from the white snow.

Precepts from the Gnomic Poets

(1) Happy is the man who loves fair lads and whole-hoofed horses and hounds for the chase and strangers from foreign lands.—SOLON.

(2) Many a knave is rich and many an honest man is poor. But never will we barter virtue for gold. Virtue lasts for ever; money flies from hand to hand.—SOLON.

(3) Speak soft words to your enemy. But when you have him under your hand, take vengeance and admit no excuse. —THEOGNIS.

(4) Too much wine is an evil. But partake thereof wisely, and it becomes a blessing instead of a curse.—THEOGNIS.

(5) I hate the gadding woman and the lecherous man who wants to plough another's field.—THEOGNIS.

(6) The best marriage for a man of sense is when the wife brings virtue as her wedding gift. That is the one dowry that keeps a household safe.—HIPPONAX.

(7) With a woman there are only two days that are truly pleasant: the day you marry her and the day you bury her.—HIPPONAX.

Women Types

SIMONIDES OF AMORGOS.

The curious strain of misogyny which so profoundly affected the conditions of society in Ionia and in Athens is continually finding expression in literature. One of its most striking manifestations is here given.

God made women's minds different from the first. One he made from a bristly pig, and in her house everything lies in disorder, bedraggled with mud or rolling about on the floor, while the mistress, unwashed and in dirty clothes, sits in the mire and waxes fat.

The second woman God made from a mischievous fox. She knows everything: nothing that is bad is hidden from her, and nothing that is good. Often her speech is fair, but often it is evil; and her temper changes from day to day.

The third sort of woman was made from a dog, and she is the true child of her mother, ever restless. She wants to hear everything and to know everything. She is always peering and roaming around, barking even though there is no one in sight. A man cannot stop her, neither with threats nor if in anger he break her teeth with a stone. Kind words are useless and it matters not to her even if she be sitting among strangers. She is a continual and a hopeless nuisance.

The fourth woman the gods in heaven fashioned from clay and then gave her half completed to man. Such a woman as this knows nothing good or bad; the only business that she understands is eating. Even if God sends bitter winter weather, though she may shiver she will not draw her chair close to the fire.

The fifth woman was made from the sea, and she has two minds within her. One day she is all smiles and gladness. A stranger in the house seeing her will sing her praise: "In all the world there is not a better or a fairer lady than this." But the next day she is dangerous to look at or approach: she is in a wild frenzy, like a bitch with her cubs, savage to all alike, friends or foes, detestable. Even as the sea stands often still and peaceful, a joy to sailors in the summer season, and often also is driven to madness with loud-thundering waves. It is to the sea that such a woman is most like.

The sixth woman was made from a stubborn grey ass. Even by force and reviling you will scarcely get her to give way and work contentedly. She is always eating, night and day: she eats in her bedroom, she eats by the fireside. But if a man comes to make love to her she welcomes his company quickly enough.

The seventh woman was made from a weasel, a plaguy and a grievous kind. In her there is nothing fair or desirable, nothing pleasant, nothing charming. As for love, she fills any man who comes near her with nausea. She is a thief and a nuisance to her neighbours, and often she gobbles up the sacrifice herself without offering anything to the gods.

The eighth woman was the daughter of a delicate long-maned mare. She shudders at the thought of servant's work or labour. She will never touch the grinding stone, nor lift the sieve, nor throw out the refuse. She will not even sit near the kitchen stove, because she is afraid of the soot, and she makes her man well acquainted with adversity. Every day, two or three times, she washes the dirt from her and anoints herself with perfumed oils. Her hair is always long and well combed, with garlands of flowers upon it. Such a woman is a fine sight for other men to see, but she is a curse to her owner, unless he be a tyrant or a sceptred king, whose heart prides itself on such delights.

The ninth woman was made from a monkey. This sort is above all others the very greatest curse that God ever sent to men. Her face is hideous. Such a woman, as she walks through a town, is a mockery for all men. She has a short neck and moves with difficulty: she has no buttocks, her legs are all bone. Alas for the poor wight who clasps such an evil thing in his arms! She knows every sort of trick and turn, and, like a monkey, she cares not for laughter. She never renders any one a service, but all day long she makes it her chief aim to do as much mischief as she can.

The tenth woman was made from a bee: happy the man who gets her! On her alone no breath of scandal lights; beneath her care the household flourishes and waxes rich. Husband and wife grow old together in love, and fair and honourable are her children. Famous is she among all women, and a divine grace surrounds her. She takes no delight in sitting with other women when they are telling each other loose stories.

Such women as this are the best and wisest wherewith God favours men. All the other sorts are a bane to men, and by God's decree a bane they always will be.

HERODOTUS

Herodotus is far more alive to the importance of social conditions than is any other Greek historian, and in this, as in most respects, offers a striking contrast to his contemporary Thucydides. The following three extracts are taken, with some revision, from Cary's translation.

Episodes in the History of a Great Family

HERODOTUS vi. 125–131.

The Alcmaeonidae were even from a very early period famous at Athens; but after the time of Alcmaeon, and later of Megacles, they became very distinguished. For, in the first place, Alcmaeon, son of Megacles, was coadjutor to the Lydians from Sardis, who came on the part of Croesus to consult the oracle of Delphi, and he assisted them zealously: and Croesus being informed by the Lydians, who had gone to consult the oracle, that he had done him good service, sent for him to Sardis; and when he arrived, presented him with so much gold as he could carry away at once on his own person. Alcmaeon, for the purpose of such a present, had recourse to the following expedient. He put on a large cloak, and having left a deep fold in it, and drawn on the widest boots he could find, he went into the treasury to which they conducted him. There coming across a heap of gold-dust, he first stuffed around his legs as much gold as the boots would contain; and then, having filled the whole fold with gold, and having sprinkled the gold-dust over the hair of his head, and put more into his mouth, he went out of the treasury, dragging his boots with difficulty, and resembling any thing rather than a man; for his mouth was stuffed, and he was all over swollen. Croesus, when he saw

22

him, burst into laughter; and he gave him all that, and besides presented him with other things not of less value than it. Thus this family became extremely rich; and this Alcmaeon, having now the means to breed horses, won the prize for four-horse chariots in the Olympic games. In the second generation after, Clisthenes, tyrant of Sicyon, raised the family, so that it became far more celebrated among the Greeks than it had been before. For Clisthenes, son of Aristonymus, son of Myron, son of Andreas, had a daughter whose name was Agarista: her he resolved to give in marriage to the man whom he should find the most accomplished of all the Greeks. When, therefore, the Olympian games were being celebrated, Clisthenes, being victorious in them in the chariot race, made a proclamation: "that whoever of the Greeks deemed himself worthy to become the son-in-law of Clisthenes, should come to Sicyon on the sixtieth day, or even before; since Clisthenes had determined on the marriage in a year, reckoning from the sixtieth day." Thereupon such of the Greeks as were puffed up with themselves and their country, came as suitors; and Clisthenes, having made a race-course and gymnasium for them, kept it for this very purpose. From Italy, accordingly, came Smindyrides, son of Hippocrates, a Sybarite, who more than any other man reached the highest pitch of luxury (and Sybaris was at that time in a most flourishing condition); and Damasus of Siris, son of Amyris called the Wise: these came from Italy. From the Ionian gulf, Amphimnestus, son of Epistrophus, an Epidamnian; he came from the Ionian gulf. An Aetolian came, Males, brother of that Titormus who surpassed the Greeks in strength, and fled from the society of men to the extremity of the Aetolian territory. And from Peloponnesus, Leocedes, son of Pheidon tyrant of the Argives, a descendant of that Pheidon who introduced measures among the Peloponnesians, and was the most

insolent of all the Greeks, who having removed the Elean
umpires, himself regulated the games at Olympia; his son
accordingly came. And Amiantus, son of Lycurgus, an
Arcadian from Trapezus; and an Azenian from the city
of Paeos, Laphanes, son of Euphorion, who, as the story is
told in Arcadia, received the Dioscuri in his house, and after
that entertained all men; and an Elean, Onomastus, son of
Agaeus: these accordingly came from the Peloponnesus
itself. From Athens there came Megacles, son of Alcmaeon,
the same who had visited Croesus, and another, Hippoclides,
son of Tisander, who surpassed the Athenians in wealth
and beauty. From Eretria, which was flourishing at that
time, came Lysanias; he was the only one from Euboea.
And from Thessaly there came, of the Scopades, Diactorides
of Crannon; and from the Molossi, Alcon. So many were
the suitors. When they had arrived on the appointed day,
Clisthenes made inquiries of their country, and the family
of each; then detaining them for a year, he made trial of
their manly qualities, their dispositions, learning, and morals;
holding familiar intercourse with each separately, and with
all together, and leading out to the gymnasia such of them
as were younger; but most of all he made trial of them at the
banquet: for as long as he detained them, he did this throughout, and at the same time entertained them magnificently.
And somehow of all the suitors those that had come from
Athens pleased him most, and of these Hippoclides, son of
Tisander, was preferred both on account of his manly
qualities, and because he was distantly related to the Cyp-
selidae in Corinth. When the day appointed for the con-
summation of the marriage arrived, and for the declaration
of Clisthenes himself, whom he would choose of them all,
Clisthenes, having sacrificed a hundred oxen, entertained
both the suitors themselves and all the Sicyonians; and when
they had concluded the feast, the suitors had a contest in

music, and general conversation. As the drinking went on, Hippoclides, who was much the most prominent, ordered the flute-player to play a dance; and when the flute-player obeyed, he began to dance: and he danced, probably, so as to please himself; but Clisthenes, seeing it, beheld the whole matter with disfavour. Afterwards, Hippoclides, having rested awhile, ordered some one to bring in a table; and when the table came in, he first danced Laconian figures on it, and then Attic ones; and in the third place, having leant his head on the table he gesticulated with his legs. But Clisthenes, when he danced the first and second time, revolted from the thought of having Hippoclides for his son-in-law, on account of his dancing and want of decorum, yet restrained himself, not wishing to burst out against him; but when he saw him gesticulating with his legs, he was no longer able to restrain himself, and said: "Son of Tisander, you have danced away your marriage." But Hippoclides answered: "No matter to Hippoclides." Hence this answer became a proverb. Clisthenes, having commanded silence, thus addressed the assembled company: "Gentlemen, suitors of my daughter, I commend you all, and, if it were possible, would gratify you all, not selecting one of you above the others, nor rejecting the rest. But as it is not possible, since I have to determine about a single damsel, to indulge the wishes of all; to such of you as are rejected from the marriage I present a talent of silver to each, on account of your condescending to take a wife from my family, and of your absence from home; but to Megacles, son of Alcmaeon, I betroth my daughter Agarista, according to the laws of the Athenians." When Megacles said that he accepted the betrothal, the marriage was celebrated by Clisthenes. This happened respecting the decision between the suitors, and thus the Alcmaeonidae became celebrated throughout Greece. From this marriage sprung Clisthenes, who established the tribes and a democracy among the Athenians, taking his name from his maternal grandfather the Sicyonian; he was born to Megacles, as was also Hippocrates: and from Hippocrates, another Megacles, and another Agarista, who took her name from Agarista, daughter of Clisthenes; she having married Xanthippus, son of Ariphron, and being with child, saw a vision in her sleep, and fancied that she brought forth a lion; and after a few days she bore Pericles to Xanthippus.

A Tyrant's Household

HERODOTUS v. 92, iii. 50–53.

The constitution of the Corinthians was formerly of this kind: it was an oligarchy, and those who were called Bacchiadae governed the city; they intermarried only within their own family. Amphion, one of these men, had a lame daughter, her name was Labda: as no one of the Bacchiadae would marry her, Eetion, son of Echecrates, who was of the district of Petra, though originally one of the Lapithae, and a descendant of Caeneus, had her. He had no children by this wife, nor by any other, and therefore went to Delphi to inquire about having offspring; and immediately as he entered, the Pythian saluted him in the following lines: "Eetion, no one honours thee, though worthy of much honour. Labda is pregnant, and will bring forth a round stone; it will fall on monarchs, and will execute justice on Corinth." This oracle, pronounced to Eetion, was by chance reported to the Bacchiadae, to whom a former oracle concerning Corinth was unintelligible, and which tended to the same end as that of Eetion, and was in these terms: "An eagle broods on rocks; and shall bring forth a lion, strong and carnivorous; and it shall loosen the knees of many. Now ponder this well, ye Corinthians, who dwell around beauteous Pirene and frowning Corinth." Now this, which had been given before, was unintelligible to the Bacchiadae; but now, when they heard that which was delivered to Eetion, they presently understood the former one, since it agreed with that given to Eetion. And though they comprehended, they kept it secret, purposing to destroy the offspring that should be born to Eetion. As soon as the woman brought forth, they sent ten of their own number to the district where Eetion lived, to put the child to death; and when they arrived at Petra, and entered Eetion's courtyard, they asked for the child; but Labda, knowing nothing of the purpose for which they had come, and supposing that they asked for it out of affection for the father, brought the child, and put it into the hands of one of them. Now, it had been determined by them on the way, that whichever of them should first receive the child, should dash it on the ground. When, however, Labda brought and gave it to one of them, the child, by a divine providence, smiled on the man who received it; and when he perceived this, a feeling of pity restrained him from killing it; and, moved by compassion, he gave it to the second, and he to the third; thus the infant, being handed from one to another, passed through the hands of all the ten, and not one of them was willing to destroy it. Having therefore delivered the child again to its mother, and gone out, they stood at the door, and attacked each other with mutual recriminations; and especially the first who took the child, because he had not done as had been determined: at last, when some time had elapsed, they determined to go in again, and that every one should share in the murder. But it was fated that misfortunes should spring up to Corinth from the progeny of Eetion. For Labda, standing at the very door, heard all that had passed; and fearing that they might change their resolution, and having obtained the child a second time might kill it, she took and hid it, in a place which appeared least likely to be thought of, in a chest; being very certain, that if they should return and come back to search, they would pry everywhere; which in fact did happen: but when, having come and made a strict search, they could not find the child, they resolved to depart, and tell those who sent them that they had done all that they had commanded. After this, Eetion's son grew up, and having escaped this danger, the name of Cypselus was given him, from the chest. When Cypselus reached man's estate, and consulted the oracle, an ambiguous answer was given him at Delphi; relying on which, he attacked and got possession of Corinth. The oracle was this: "Happy this man, who is come down to my dwelling; Cypselus, son of Eetion, king of renowned Corinth; he and his children, but not his children's children." Such was the oracle. And Cypselus, having obtained the tyranny, behaved himself thus: he banished many of the Corinthians, deprived many of their property, and many more of their life. When he had reigned thirty years, and ended his life happily, his son Periander became his successor in the tyranny. Now Periander at first was more mild than his father; but when he had communicated by ambassadors with Thrasybulus, tyrant of Miletus, he became far more cruel than Cypselus. For having sent a nuncio to Thrasybulus, he asked in what way, having ordered affairs most securely, he might best govern the city. Thrasybulus conducted the person who came from Periander out of the city, and going into a field of corn, and as he went through the standing corn, questioning him about, and making him repeat over again, the account of his coming from Corinth, he cut off any ear that he saw taller than the rest, and having cut it off, he threw it away, till in this manner he had destroyed the best and deepest of the corn. Having gone through the piece of ground, and given no message at all, he dismissed the nuncio. When the nuncio returned to

Corinth, Periander was anxious to know the answer of Thrasybulus; but he said that Thrasybulus had given him no answer, and wondered he should have sent him to such a man, for that he was crazy, and destroyed his own property, relating what he had seen done by Thrasybulus. But Periander, comprehending the meaning of the action, and understanding that Thrasybulus advised him to put to death the most eminent of the citizens, thereupon exercised all manner of cruelties towards his subjects; for whatever Cypselus had left undone, by killing and banishing, Periander completed. One day he stripped all the Corinthian women, on account of his own wife Melissa: for when he sent messengers to the Thesprotians on the river Acheron, to consult the oracle of the dead respecting a deposit made by a stranger, Melissa having appeared, said that she would neither make it known, nor tell in what place the deposit lay, because she was cold and naked; for that there was no use in the garments in which he had buried her, since they had not been burnt: and as a proof that she spoke truth, she added that Periander had put his bread into a cold oven. When this answer was brought back to Periander, for the token was convincing to him, since he had lain with Melissa after her death, he immediately, on receiving the message, made proclamation that all the women of Corinth should repair to the temple of Juno. They accordingly went, as to a festival, dressed in their best attire; but he having privately introduced his guards, stripped them all alike, both the free women and attendants; and having collected their clothes in a pit, he invoked Melissa, and burnt them. When he had done this, and sent a second time, the phantom of Melissa told in what place she had laid the stranger's deposit.

. . . . . .

When Periander had killed his own wife Melissa, it

happened that another calamity succeeded the former. He
had two sons by Melissa, one seventeen, the other eighteen
years of age. These their maternal grandfather, Procles,
who was tyrant of Epidaurus, sent for, and treated affection-
ately, as was natural, they being the sons of his own daughter.
But when he sent them home, as he escorted them on their
way, he said, "Do you know, my sons, who killed your
mother?" The elder of them took no notice of these words;
but the younger, whose name was Lycophron, when he
heard it, was so grieved at hearing this, that on his return at
Corinth, he neither addressed his father, regarding him as
the murderer of his mother, nor entered into conversation
with him, nor answered a word to his questions. At last
Periander, being exceedingly angry, drove him from the
palace. Having driven him out, he inquired of the elder one
what their grandfather had said to them. He related to him
how kindly he had received them; but he did not mention
the words Procles said as he was escorting them, for he had
paid no attention to them. But Periander affirmed that it
was impossible but that he had suggested something to them;
and he persevered in his inquiries, till the young man recovered his memory, and mentioned this also. Periander,
reflecting on this, and resolving not to show any indulgence,
sent a messenger to the persons by whom the son who was
driven out was entertained, and forbade them to receive him
in their houses. So he, when being driven out from one house
he came to another, was driven from this also, since Periander
threatened all that received him, and required them to expel
him. Being thus driven about, he went to some other of his
friends; and they, though in dread, yet received him as the
son of Periander. At last Periander made a proclamation,
that whoever should either receive him in his house, or
converse with him, should pay a sacred fine to Apollo,
mentioning the amount. In consequence of this proclamation,

therefore, no one would either converse with him, or receive him into their houses; besides he himself did not think it right to attempt what was forbidden, but persisting in his purpose lived as a vagrant among the porticoes. On the fourth day Periander, seeing him reduced to a state of filth and starvation, felt compassion, and relaxing his anger approached him, and said, " My son, which of these is preferable, your present mode of life, or by accommodating yourself to your father's wishes, to succeed to the power and riches which I now possess? You, who are my son, and a prince of wealthy Corinth, have chosen a vagabond life, by opposing and showing anger towards him whom, least of all, you ought so to treat. For if any calamity has occurred in our family on account of which you have conceived disfavour towards me, it has fallen upon me chiefly, and I bear the chief burden of it, inasmuch as I did the deed. Do you, therefore, having learnt how much better it is to be envied than pitied, and at the same time what it is to be angry with parents and superiors, return to your home." With these words Periander endeavoured to restrain him. He, however, gave his father no other answer, but said that he had made himself liable to pay the sacred fine to the god, by having spoken to him. Periander therefore perceiving that the distemper of his son was impracticable and invincible, put him on board a ship, and sent him out of his sight to Corcyra, for he was also master of that island. Periander having sent him away, made war on his father-in-law, Procles, as being the principal author of the present troubles; and he took Epidaurus, and took Procles himself and kept him prisoner. But when, in lapse of time, Periander grew old, and became conscious that he was no longer able to superintend and manage public affairs, having sent to Corcyra, he recalled Lycophron to assume the government, for he did not perceive in his eldest son any capacity for

D

government, but he appeared to him dull of intellect. But
Lycophron did not deign to give an answer to the bearer of
the message. Nevertheless Periander, having a strong affection
for the youth, next sent to him his sister, who was his own
daughter, thinking she would be most likely to persuade him.
On her arrival she thus addressed him: "Brother, would
you that the government should pass to others, and that
your father's family should be utterly destroyed, rather than
yourself return and possess it? Come home, then, and cease
to punish yourself. Obstinacy is a sorry possession: think
not to cure one evil by another. Many have preferred equity
to strict justice; and many, ere this, in seeking their mother's
rights have lost their father's inheritance. A kingdom is an
uncertain possession, and many are suitors for it. He is now
old, and past the vigour of life. Do not give your own to
others." Thus she, having been instructed by her father,
said what was most likely to persuade him. But he in answer
said, that he would never return to Corinth so long as he
should hear his father was living. When she brought back
this answer, Periander sent a third time by a herald to say,
that he himself intended to go to Corcyra; and urged him
to return to Corinth, and become his successor in the kingdom. The son consenting to this proposal, Periander pre
pared to set out for Corcyra, and his son for Corinth; but
the Corcyraeans being informed of each particular, in order
that Periander might not come to their country, killed the
young man: and in return for this, Periander took vengeance
on the Corcyraeans.

A Scandal at Sparta

HERODOTUS vi. 61–69

At that time, therefore, while Cleomenes was at Aegina,
and co-operating for the common good of Greece, Demaratus

accused him; not so much caring for the Aeginetae, as moved by envy and hatred. But Cleomenes, having returned from Aegina, formed a plan to deprive Demaratus of the sovereignty, getting a handle against him by means of the following circumstance. Ariston, king of Sparta, had married two wives, but he had no children; and as he did not acknowledge himself to be the cause of this, he married a third wife; and he married her in this manner. He had a friend, who was a Spartan, to whom he was more attached than to any other of the citizens. The wife of this man happened to be by far the most beautiful of all the women in Sparta, and this moreover, having become the most beautiful from being the most ugly. For her nurse perceiving that she was misshapen, and knowing her to be the daughter of opulent persons, and deformed, and seeing moreover that her parents considered her appearance a great misfortune, considering these several circumstances, devised the following plan. She carried her every day to the temple of Helen, which is in the place called Therapne, above the temple of Phoebus. When the nurse brought the child there, she stood before the image, and entreated the goddess to free the child from its deformity. And it is related, that one day as the nurse was going out of the temple, a woman appeared to her, and having appeared, asked what she was carrying in her arms; and she answered, that she was carrying an infant; whereupon she bid her show it to her, but the nurse refused, for she had been forbidden by the parents to show the child to any one; the woman, however, urged her by all means to show it to her, and the nurse, seeing that the woman was so very anxious to see the child, at length showed it; upon which she, stroking the head of the child with her hands, said that she would surpass all the women of Sparta in beauty; and from that day her appearance began to change. When she reached the age for marriage, Agetus, son of Alcides, married her; this, then was the friend of Ariston. Now love for this woman excited Ariston; he therefore had recourse to the following stratagem. He promised he would give his friend, whose wife this woman was, a present of any one thing he should choose out of all his possessions, and required his friend in return to do the like to him. He, having no apprehension on account of his wife, seeing that Ariston already had a wife, assented to the proposal; and they imposed oaths on each other on these terms. Accordingly Ariston himself gave the thing, whatever it was, which Agetus chose out of all his treasures; and himself claiming to obtain the same compliance from him, thereupon attempted to carry off his wife with him. Agetus said that he had assented to any thing but this only; nevertheless, being compelled by his oath, and circumvented by deceit, he suffered him to take her away with him. Thus, then, Ariston took to himself a third wife, having put away the second. But in too short a time, and before she had completed her ten months, this woman bore Demaratus; and as he was sitting on the bench with the Ephors, one of his servants announced to him that a son was born to him; but he, knowing the time at which he married the woman, and reckoning the months on his fingers, said with an oath, "It cannot be mine." This the Ephors heard. However, at the time, they took no notice. The child grew up, and Ariston repented of what he had said, for he was fully persuaded that Demaratus was his son. He gave him the name of Demaratus for this reason; before this the Spartans had made public supplications, that Ariston, whom they esteemed the most illustrious of all the kings that had ever reigned in Sparta, might have a son. For this reason the name of Demaratus was given to him. In process of time Ariston died, and Demaratus obtained the sovereignty. But it was fated, as it appears, that these things, when made known, should occasion the deposition of Demaratus from

the sovereignty, for Demaratus had incurred the hatred of
Cleomenes, because he had before led away the army from
Eleusis, and now more particularly when Cleomenes had
crossed over against those Aeginetans who were inclined to
Medism. Cleomenes then, being eager to avenge himself,
made a compact with Leutychides, son of Menares, son of
Agis, who was of the same family with Demaratus, on
condition, that if he should make him king instead of
Demaratus, he should accompany him against the Aeginetans.
Leutychides had become an enemy to Demaratus, chiefly
for this reason. When Leutychides was affianced to Percalus,
daughter of Chilon, son of Demarmenus, Demaratus, having
plotted against him, disappointed Leutychides of his marriage; having himself anticipated him by seizing Percalus
and retaining her as his wife. In this manner the enmity of
Leutychides to Demaratus originated, and now, at the
instigation of Cleomenes, Leutychides made oath against
Demaratus, affirming "that he did not legitimately reign
over the Spartans, not being the son of Ariston"; and after
making oath against him, he prosecuted him, recalling the
words which Ariston spoke, when the servant announced
that a son was born to him, whereupon he, reckoning the
months, denied with an oath, saying, "that it was not his."
Leutychides, insisting on this declaration, maintained that
Demaratus was neither the son of Ariston, nor rightful king
of Sparta; and he adduced as witnesses those Ephors who
were then sitting by the king, and heard these words of
Ariston. At length, the matter coming to a trial, the Spartans
determined to inquire of the oracle at Delphi, " whether
Demaratus was the son of Ariston." But the matter being
referred to the Pythian at the instance of Cleomenes, Cleomenes thereupon gained over one Cobon, son of Aristo-
phantus, a man of very great influence at Delphi: and Cobon
prevailed with Perialla the prophetess to say what Cleomenes

wished to be said. The Pythian accordingly, when the persons
sent to consult the oracle made the inquiry, decided that
Demaratus was not the son of Ariston. In after time this
came to be known, and Cobon fled from Delphi, and Perialla
the prophetess was deposed from her office.

Thus, then, it happened with respect to the deposition of
Demaratus from the sovereignty; and he fled from Sparta
to the Medes on account of the following insult. After his
deposition from the sovereignty, he was chosen to and held
the office of magistrate. The Gymnopaediae were being
celebrated; and, when Demaratus was looking on, Leutychides, who had been appointed king in his room, sent a
servant and asked him, by way of ridicule and mockery,
"what kind of thing it was to be a magistrate after having
been a king?" But he, being vexed with the question,
answered, "that he indeed had tried both, but Leutychides
had not; however, that this question would be the com-
mencement either of infinite calamity or infinite prosperity
to the Lacedaemonians." Having spoken thus and covered
his face, he went out of the theatre to his own house; and
having immediately made preparation, he sacrificed an ox to
Zeus, and having sacrificed, called for his mother. When
his mother came, he placed part of the entrails in her hands,
and supplicated her, speaking as follows: "Mother, I beseech you, calling to witness both the rest of the gods, and
especially our household divinity, to tell me the truth, who
is in reality my father? For Leutychides affirmed on the trial,
that you being pregnant by your former husband, so came
to Ariston; others tell even a more idle story, and say you
kept company with one of the servants, a feeder of asses, and
that I am his son. I adjure you therefore by the gods to speak
the truth: for even if you have done any thing of what is
said, you have not done it alone, but with many others;
moreover, the report is common in Sparta, that Ariston

was incapable of begetting children, for that otherwise his former wives would have had offspring." Thus he spoke. She answered as follows: "Son, since you implore me with supplications to speak the truth, the whole truth shall be told you. When Ariston had taken me to his own house, on the third night from the first, a spectre resembling Ariston came to me; and having lain with me, put on me a crown that it had: it departed, and afterwards Ariston came; but when he saw me with the crown, he asked who it was that gave it me. I said, he did; but he would not admit it; whereupon I took an oath, and said that he did not well to deny it, for that having come shortly before and lain with me, he had given me the crown. Ariston, seeing that I affirmed with an oath, discovered that the event was superhuman: and in the first place, the crown proved to have come from the shrine situate near the palace gates, which they call Astrobacus's; and in the next place, the seers pronounced that it was the hero himself. Thus, then, my son, you have all that you wish to know: for you are sprung either from that hero, and the hero Astrobacus is your father, or Ariston; for I conceived you in that night. As to that with which your enemies most violently attack you, affirming that Ariston himself, when your birth was announced to him, in the presence of many persons, denied you were his, for that the time, ten months, had not yet elapsed; he threw out those words through ignorance of such matters; for women bring forth at nine months and seven, and all do not complete ten months. But I bore you, my son, at seven months: and Ariston himself knew, not long after, that he had uttered those words thoughtlessly. Do not listen to any other stories respecting your birth; for you have heard the whole truth. And from feeders of asses may their wives bring forth children to Leutychides and such as spread such reports."

CARY.

ATHENS IN THE FIFTH AND
FOURTH CENTURIES

ATHENS IN THE FIFTH AND FOURTH CENTURIES

ARISTOPHANES

There is scarcely one of Aristophanes' extant eleven comedies which does not teem with allusions to the private life of his contemporaries, and the following extracts represent only a very scanty gleaning from a very plentiful harvest.

A Festival Procession

ACHARNIANS 237-279.

Enter Dicaeopolis, his Wife and Daughter, a Slave, etc.

Dicaeopolis. Peace, Peace.
          Silence, Silence.
Chorus. Stand aside! Keep out of sight! List to the sacrificial
          cries!
  There he comes, the very fellow, going out to sacrifice.
  Wait and watch him for a minute, we shall have him by
          surprise.
Dicaeopolis. Silence! move forward, the Canephora;
  You, Xanthias, follow close behind her there,
  In a proper manner, with your pole and emblem.
Wife. Set down the basket, daughter, and begin
  The ceremony.
Daughter.   Give me the cruet, mother,
  And let me pour it upon the holy cake.
Dicaeopolis. Oh, blessed Bacchus, what a joy it is
  To go thus unmolested, undisturbed,
  My wife, my children, and my family,

With our accustomed joyful ceremony,
To celebrate thy festival in my farm.
Well, here's success to the truce of thirty years.
Wife. Mind your behaviour, child; carry the basket
In a modest proper manner; look demure
And grave; a happy fellow will he be
That gives more than an eye to ye.—Come, move on.
Mind your gold trinkets, they'll be stolen else.
Dicaeopolis. Follow behind there, Xanthias, with the pole,
And I'll strike up the bacchanalian chant.
Wife, you must be spectator; go within,
And mount to the housetop to behold us pass.
Dicaeopolis [*sings*]. Leader of the revel rout,
Of the drunken roar and shout,
Crazy mirth and saucy jesting,
Frolic and intrigue clandestine!
Half a dozen years are passed,
Here we meet in peace at last.
All my wars and fights are o'er:
Other battles please me more,
With my neighbour's maid, the Thracian,
Found marauding in the wood;
Seizing on the fair occasion,
With a quick retaliation
Making an immediate booty
Of her innocence and beauty.
If a drunken head should ache,
Bones and heads we never break.
If we quarrel overnight,
At a full carousing soak,
In the morning all is right;
And the shield hung out of sight
In the chimney smoke.

The Plain Man on War

ACHARNIANS 496–556.

Dicaeopolis. Be not surprised, most excellent spectators,
  If I, that am a beggar, have presumed
  To claim an audience upon public matters
  Even in a comedy; for comedy
  Is conversant in all the rules of justice,
  And can distinguish betwixt right and wrong.
    The words I speak are bold, but just and true.
  Cleon, at least, cannot accuse me now,
  That I defame the city before strangers.
  For this is the Lenaean festival,
  And here we meet, all by ourselves alone;
  No deputies are arrived as yet with tribute,
  No strangers or allies; but here we sit
  A chosen sample, clean as sifted corn,
  With our own denizens as a kind of chaff.
    First, I detest the Spartans most extremely;
  And wish, that Neptune, the Taenarian deity,
  Would bury them in their houses with his earthquakes.
  For I've had losses—losses, let me tell ye,
  Like other people; vines cut down and injured.
  But, among friends (for only friends are here),
  Why should we blame the Spartans for all this?
  For people of ours, some people of our own,
  Some people from amongst us here, I mean;
  But not the people (pray remember that);
  I never said the people—but a pack
  Of paltry people, mere pretended citizens,
  Base counterfeits, went laying informations,
  And making a confiscation of the jerkins
  Imported here from Megara; pigs moreover,
  Pumpkins, and pecks of salt, and ropes of onions,

Were voted to be merchandise from Megara,
Denounced, and seized, and sold upon the spot.
    Well, these might pass, as petty local matters.
But now, behold, some doughty drunken youths
Kidnap, and carry away from Megara,
The courtesan Simaetha. Those of Megara,
In hot retaliation, seize a brace
Of equal strumpets, hurried forth perforce
From Dame Aspasia's house of recreation.
So this was the beginning of the war,
All over Greece, owing to these three strumpets.
For Pericles, like an Olympian Jove,
With all his thunder and his thunderbolts,
Began to storm and lighten dreadfully,
Alarming all the neighbourhood of Greece;
And made decrees, drawn up like drinking songs,
In which it was enacted and concluded,
That the Megarians should remain excluded
From every place where commerce was transacted,
With all their ware—like "old care"—in the ballad:
And this decree, by land and sea, was valid.
    Then the Megarians, being all half starved,
Desired the Spartans, to desire of us,
Just to repeal those laws; the laws I mentioned,
Occasioned by the stealing of those strumpets.
And so they begged and prayed us several times;
And we refused; and so they went to war.
You'll say " They should not." Why, what should they
        have done?
Just make it your own case; suppose the Spartans
Had manned a boat, and landed on your islands,
And stolen a pug puppy from Seriphos;
Would you then have remained at home inglorious?
Not so, by no means; at the first report,

You would have launched at once three hundred galleys,
And filled the city with the noise of troops;
And crews of ships, crowding and clamouring
About the muster-masters and pay-masters;
With measuring corn out at the magazine,
And all the porch choked with the multitude;
With figures of Minerva, newly furbished,
Painted and gilt, parading in the streets;
With wineskins, kegs, and firkins, leeks and onions;
With garlic crammed in pouches, nets, and pokes;
With garlands, singing-girls, and bloody noses.
Our arsenal would have sounded and resounded
With bangs and thwacks of driving bolts and nails;
With shaping oars, and holes to put the oar in;
With hacking, hammering, clattering, and boring;
Words of command, whistles and pipes and fifes.
    "Such would have been your conduct. Will you say,
That Telephus should have acted otherwise?"

The Market

ACHARNIANS 719–928.

Dicaeopolis. Well, there's the boundary of my market-place,
    Marked out, for the Peloponnesians and Boeotians
    And the Megarians. All are freely welcome
    To traffic and sell with me, but not with Lamachus.
    Moreover I've appointed constables,
    With lawful and sufficient straps and thongs,
    To keep the peace, and to coerce and punish
    All spies and vagabonds and informing people.
    Come, now for the column, with the terms of peace
    Inscribed upon it! I must fetch it out,
    And fix it here in the centre of my market.   [*Exit.*

Enter a Megarian with his two little Girls.

Megarian. Ah, there's the Athenian market! Heaven bless it,
　I say; the welcomest sight to a Megarian.
　I've looked for it, and longed for it, like a child
　For its own mother. You, my daughters dear,
　Disastrous offspring of a dismal sire,
　List to my words; and let them sink impressed
　Upon your empty stomachs; now's the time
　That you must seek a livelihood for yourselves.
　Therefore resolve at once, and answer me;
　Will you be sold abroad, or starve at home?
Both. Let us be sold, papa! Let us be sold!
Megarian. I say so too; but who do ye think will purchase
　Such useless mischievous commodities?
　However, I have a notion of my own,
　A true Megarian scheme; I mean to sell ye
　Disguised as pigs, with artificial pettitoes.
　Here, take them, and put them on. Remember now,
　Show yourselves off; do credit to your breeding,
　Like decent pigs; or else, by Mercury,
　If I'm obliged to take you back to Megara,
　There you shall starve, far worse than heretofore.
　—This pair of masks too—fasten 'em on your faces,
　And crawl into the sack there on the ground.
　Mind ye—Remember—you must squeak and whine,
　And racket about like little roasting pigs.
　—And I'll call out for Dicaeopolis.
　Ho, Dicaeopolis, Dicaeopolis!
　I say, would you please to buy some pigs of mine?
Dicaeopolis. What's there? a Megarian?
Megarian [*sneakingly*].　　　Yes—We're come to market.
Dicaeopolis. How goes it with you?
Megarian.　　　　　　We're all like to starve.

Dicaeopolis. Well, liking is everything. If you have your
        liking,
  That's all in all: the likeness is a good one,
  A pretty likeness! like to starve, you say.
  But what else are you doing?
Megarian.   What we're doing?
  I left our governing people all contriving
  To ruin us utterly without loss of time.
Dicaeopolis. It's the only way; it will keep you out of mischief,
  Meddling and getting into scrapes.
Megarian.   Aye, yes.
Dicaeopolis. Well, what's your other news? How's corn?
  What price?
Megarian. Corn? it's above all price; we worship it.
Dicaeopolis. But salt? You've salt, I reckon—
Megarian.   Salt? how should we?
  Have you not seized the salt pans?
Dicaeopolis.   No! nor garlic?
  Have not ye garlic?
Megarian.   What do ye talk of garlic?
  As if you had not wasted and destroyed it,
  And grubbed the very roots out of the ground.
Dicaeopolis. Well, what have you got then? Tell us! Can't ye!
Megarian [*in the tone of a sturdy resolute lie*]. Pigs—
  Pigs truly—pigs forsooth, for sacrifice.
Dicaeopolis. That's well, let's look at 'em.
Megarian.   Aye, they're handsome ones;
  You may feel how heavy they are, if ye hold 'em up.
Dicaeopolis. Hey-day! What's this? What's here?
Megarian.   A pig, to be sure.
Dicaeopolis. Do ye say so? Where does it come from?
Megarian.   Come? from Megara.
  What, an't it a pig?
Dicaeopolis.   No truly, it does not seem so.

E

Megarian. Did you ever hear the like? Such an unaccountable,
    Suspicious fellow! it is not a pig, he says!
    But I'll be judged; I'll bet ye a bushel of salt,
    It's what we call a natural proper pig.
Dicaeopolis. Perhaps it may, but it's a human pig.
Megarian. Human! I'm human; and they're mine, that's all.
    Whose should they be, do ye think? so far they're human.
    But come, will you hear 'em squeak?
Dicaeopolis.   Aye, yes, by Jove,
With all my heart.
Megarian.   Come now, pig! now's the time:
    Remember what I told ye—squeak directly!
    Squeak, can't ye? Curse ye, what's the matter with ye?
    Squeak when I bid you, I say; by Mercury,
    I'll carry you back to Megara if you don't.
Daughter. Wee wée.
Megarian.   Do ye hear the pig?
Dicaeopolis.   The pig, do ye call it?
    It will be a different creature before long.
Megarian. It will take after the mother, like enough.
Dicaeopolis. Aye, but this pig won't do for sacrifice.
Megarian. Why not? Why won't it do for sacrifice?
Dicaeopolis. Imperfect! here's no tail!
Megarian.   Poh, never mind;
    It will have a tail in time, like all the rest.
    But feel this other, just the fellow to it;
    With a little further keeping, it would serve
    For a pretty dainty sacrifice to Venus.
Dicaeopolis. You warrant 'em weaned? they'll feed without
           the mother?
Megarian. Without the mother or the father either.
Dicaeopolis. But what do they like to eat?
Megarian.   Just what ye give 'em;
    You may ask 'em if you will.

Dicaeopolis.   Pig, Pig!

1st Daughter.   Wee wée.

Dicaeopolis. Pig, are ye fond of peas?

1st Daughter.   Wee wée, Wee wée.

Dicaeopolis. Are ye fond of figs?

1st Daughter.   Wee wée, Wee wée, Wee wée.

Dicaeopolis. You little one, are you fond of figs?

2nd Daughter.   Wee wée.

Dicaeopolis. What a squeak was there! they're ravenous for
        the figs;
  Go, somebody, fetch out a parcel of figs
  For the little pigs! Heh, what, they'll eat I warrant.
  Lawk there, look at 'em racketing and bustling!
  How they do munch and crunch! in the name of heaven,
  Why, sure they can't have eaten 'em all already!

Megarian [*sneakingly*]. Not all, there's this one here, I took
        myself.

Dicaeopolis. Well, faith, they're clever comical animals.
  What shall I give you for 'em? What do ye ask?

Megarian. I must have a gross of onions for this here;
  And the other you may take for a peck of salt.

Dicaeopolis. I'll keep 'em; wait a moment.   [*Exit.*

Megarian.   Heaven be praised!
  O blessed Mercury, if I could but manage
  To make such another bargain for my wife,
  I'ld do it to-morrow, or my mother either.

Enter Informer.

Informer. Fellow, from whence?

Megarian.   From Megara with my pigs.

Informer. Then I denounce your pigs, and you yourself,
  As belonging to the enemy.

Megarian.   There it is!
  The beginning of all our troubles over again.

Informer. I'll teach you to come Megarising here:
    Let go of the sack there.
Megarian.   Dicaeopolis!
    Ho, Dicaeopolis! there's a fellow here
    Denouncing me.
Dicaeopolis.   Denouncing, is he? Constables,
    Why don't you keep the market clear of sycophants?
    You fellow, I must inform ye, your informing
    Is wholly illegal and informal here.
Informer. What, giving informations against the enemy;
    Is that prohibited?
Dicaeopolis.   At your peril! Carry
    Your information to some other market.
Megarian. What a plague it is at Athens, this informing!
Dicaeopolis. O never fear, Megarian; take it there,
    The payment for your pigs, the salt and onions:
    And fare you well.
Megarian.   That's not the fashion amongst us.
    We've not been used to faring well.
Dicaeopolis.   No matter.
    If it's offensive, I'll revoke the wish;
    And imprecate it on myself instead.   [*Exit.*
Megarian. There now, my little pigs, you must contrive
    To munch your bread with salt, if you can get it. [*Exit.*

Chorus. Our friend's affairs improve apace; his lucky
                  speculation
Is raising him to wealth and place, to name and reputation.
        With a revenue neat and clear,
        Arising without risk or fear,
        No sycophant will venture here
          To spoil his occupation.
Not Ctesias, the dirty spy, that lately terrified him;
Nor Prepis, with his infamy, will jostle side beside him:

Clothed in a neat and airy dress,
He'll move at ease among the press,
Without a fear of nastiness,
    Or danger to betide him.
Hyperbolus will never dare to indict him nor arrest him.
Cleonymus will not be there to bother and molest him.
    Nor he, the bard of little price,
    Cratinus, with the curls so nice,
    Cratinus in the new device
      In which the barber dressed him.
Nor he, the paltry saucy rogue, the poor and undeserving
Lysistratus, that heads the vogue, in impudence unswerving,
    Taunt and offence in all he says;
    Ruined in all kinds of ways;
    In every month of thirty days,
      Nine and twenty starving.

Enter a Theban with his attendants, all bearing burdens,
    followed by a train of bagpipers.

Theban. Good troth, I'm right down shoulder-galled; my lads,
    Set down your bundles. You, take care o' the herbs.
    Gently, be sure don't bruise 'em; and now, you minstrels,
    That needs would follow us all the way from Thebes,
    Blow wind i' the tail of your bagpipes, puff away.
Dicaeopolis. Get out! what wind has brought 'em here, I
      wonder?
    A parcel of hornets buzzing about the door!
    You humble-bumble drones—Get out! Get out!
Theban. As Iolaus shall help me, that's well done,
    Friend, and I thank you;—coming out of Thebes,
    They blew me away the blossom of all these herbs.
    You've sarved 'em right. So now would you please to buy,
    What likes you best, of all my chaffer here;
    All kinds, four-footed things and feathered fowl.

Dicaeopolis [*suddenly, with the common trick of condescension,*
   as if he had not observed him before].
 My little tight Boeotian! Welcome kindly,
 My little pudding-eater! What have you brought?
Theban. In a manner, everything, as a body may say;
 All the good cheer of Thebes, and the primest wares,
 Mats, trefoil, wicks for lamps, sweet marjoram,
 Coots, didappers, and water-hens—what not?
 Widgeon and teal.
Dicaeopolis.   Why, you're come here amongst us,
 Like a north wind in winter, with your wild fowl.
Theban. Moreover I've brought geese, and hares moreover,
 And eels from the lake Copais, which is more.
Dicaeopolis. O thou bestower of the best spitchcocks
 That ever yet were given to mortal man,
 Permit me to salute those charming eels.
Theban [*addressing the eel, and delivering it to Dicaeopolis*].
 Daughter, come forth, and greet the courteous stranger,
 First-born of fifty damsels of the lake!
Dicaeopolis. O long regretted and recovered late,
 Welcome, thrice welcome to the Comic Choir;
 Welcome to me, to Morychus, and all
 (Ye slaves, prepare the chafing dish and stove).
 Children, behold her here, the best of eels,
 The loveliest and the best, at length returned
 After six years of absence. I myself
 Will furnish you with charcoal for her sake.
 Salute her with respect, and wait upon
 Her entrance there within, with due conveyance.
  [*The eel is here carried off by Dicaeopolis's servants.*]
 Grant me, ye gods! so to possess thee still,
 While my life lasts, and at my latest hour,
 Fresh even and sweet as now, with . . . savoury sauce.
Theban. But how am I to be paid for it? Won't you tell me?

Dicaeopolis. Why, with respect to the eel, in the present
        instance,
  I mean to take it as a perquisite,
  As a kind of toll to the market; you understand me.
  These other things of course are meant for sale.
Theban. Yes, sure. I sell 'em all.
Dicaeopolis.   Well, what do you ask?
  Or would you take commodities in exchange?
Theban. Aye; think of something of your country produce,
  That's plentiful down here, and scarce up there.
Dicaeopolis. Well, you shall take our pilchards or our pottery.
Theban. Pilchards and pottery! Naugh, we've plenty of them.
  But think of something, as I said before,
  That's plentiful down here, and scarce up there.
Dicaeopolis [*after a moment's reflection*].
  I have it! A true-bred sycophant and informer.
  I'll give you one, tied neatly and corded up,
  Like an oil-jar.
Theban.   Aye; that's fair; by the holy twins!
  He'd bring in money, I warrant, money enough,
  Amongst our folks at home, with showing him,
  Like a mischiéf-full kind of a foreign ape.
Dicaeopolis. Well, there's Nicarchus moving down this way,
  Laying his informations. There he comes.
Theban [*contemplating him with the eye of a purchaser*].
  'A seems but a small one to look at.
Dicaeopolis.   Aye, but I promise ye
  He's full of tricks and roguery, every inch of him.

Enter Nicarchus.

Nicarchus [*in the pert peremptory tone of his profession as an
      informer*].
  Whose goods are these? these articles?
Theban.   Mine, sure;

We be come here from Thebes.

Nicarchus.   Then I denounce them
    As enemies' property.

Theban [*with an immediate outcry*]. Why, what harm have
        they done,
    The birds and creatures? Why do you quarrel with 'em?

Nicarchus. And I'll denounce you too.

Theban.   What, me? What for?

Nicarchus. To satisfy the bystanders, I'll explain.
    You've brought in wicks of lamps from an enemy's country.

Dicaeopolis [*ironically*]. And so, you bring 'em to *light*?

Nicarchus.   I bring to light
    A plot!—a plot to burn the arsenal!

Dicaeopolis [*ironically*]. With the wick of a lamp?

Nicarchus.   Undoubtedly.

Dicaeopolis.   In what way?

Nicarchus [*with great gravity*]. Boeotian might be capable
        of fixing it
    On the back of a cockroach, who might float with it
    Into the arsenal, with a north-east wind;
    And if once the fire caught hold of a single vessel,
    The whole would be in a blaze.

Dicaeopolis [*seizing hold of him*].   You dog! You villain!
    Would a cockroach burn the ships and the arsenal?

Nicarchus. Bear witness, all of ye.

Dicaeopolis.   There, stop his mouth;
    And bring me a band of straw to bind him up;
    And send him safely away, for fear of damage,
    Gently and steadily, like a potter's jar.

Rival Politicians

THE KNIGHTS 247–497.

During the last lines the Chorus of Cavaliers with their hobby-horses have entered and occupied their position in the orchestra. They begin their attack upon Cleon.

Chorus. Close around him, and confound him, the confounder
of us all.

Pelt him, pummel him and maul him; rummage, ransack,
overhaul him,

Overbear him and out-bawl him; bear him down and bring
him under.

Bellow like a burst of thunder, robber! harpy! sink of
plunder!

Rogue and villain! rogue and cheat! rogue and villain, I
repeat!

Oftener than I can repeat it, has the rogue and villain
cheated.

Close around him left and right; spit upon him; spurn and
smite:

Spit upon him as you see; spurn and spit at him like me.

But beware, or he'll evade ye, for he knows the private
track,

Where Eucrates was seen escaping with the mill dust on
his back.

Cleon. Worthy veterans of the jury, you that either right or
wrong,

With my threepenny provision, I've maintained and
cherished long,

Come to my aid! I'm here waylaid—assassinated and
betrayed!

Chorus. Rightly served! we serve you rightly, for your
hungry love of pelf,

For your gross and greedy rapine, gormandising by yourself;

You that ere the figs are gathered, pilfer with a privy twitch
Fat delinquents and defaulters, pulpy, luscious, plump, and
    rich;
Pinching, fingering, and pulling—tampering, selecting,
    culling.
With a nice survey discerning, which are green and which
    are turning,
Which are ripe for accusation, forfeiture, and confiscation.
    Him besides, the wealthy man, retired upon an easy rent,
Hating and avoiding party, noble-minded, indolent,
Fearful of official snares, intrigues and intricate affairs;
Him you mark; you fix and hook him, whilst he's gaping
    unawares;
At a fling, at once you bring him hither from the
    Chersonese,
Down you cast him, roast and baste him, and devour him
    at your case.

Cleon. Yes! assault, insult, abuse me! this is the return, I find,
For the noble testimony, the memorial I designed:
Meaning to propose proposals, for a monument of stone,
On the which, your late achievements should be carved
    and neatly done.

Chorus. Out, away with him! the slave! the pompous empty
    fawning knave!
Does he think with idle speeches to delude and cheat us all?
As he does the doting elders, that attend his daily call?
Pelt him here, and bang him there; and here and there and
    everywhere.

Cleon. Save me, neighbours! O the monsters! O my side,
    my back, my breast!

Chorus. What, you're forced to call for help? You brutal
    overbearing pest.

Sausage-seller. I'll astound you with my voice; with my
    bawling looks and noise.

Chorus. If in bawling you surpass him, you'll achieve a
victor's crown;
If again you overmatch him in impudence, the day's our
own.

Cleon. I denounce this traitor here, for sailing on clandestine
trips,
With supplies of tripe and stuffing, to careen the Spartan
ships.

Sausage-seller. I denounce then and accuse him, for a greater
worse abuse:
That he steers his empty paunch, and anchors at the public
board:
Running in without a lading, to return completely stored!

Chorus. Yes! and smuggles out, moreover, loaves and
luncheons not a few,
More than ever Pericles, in all his pride, presumed to do.

Cleon [*in a thundering tone*]. Dogs and villains, you shall die!

Sausage-seller [*in a louder, shriller tone*]. Aye! I can scream
ten times as high.

Cleon. I'll overbear ye, and out-bawl ye.

Sausage-seller. But I'll out-scream ye, and out-squall ye.

Cleon. I'll impeach you, whilst aboard,
Commanding on a foreign station.

Sausage-seller. I'll have you sliced, and slashed, and scored.

Cleon. Your lion's skin of reputation
Shall be flayed off your back and tanned.

Sausage-seller. I'll take those guts of yours in hand.

Cleon. Come, bring your eyes and mine to meet!
And stare at me without a wink!

Sausage-seller. Yes! in the market-place and street,
I had my birth and breeding too;
And from a boy, to blush or blink,
I scorn the thing as much as you.

Cleon. I'll denounce you if you mutter.

Sausage-seller. I'll douse ye the first word you utter.
Cleon. My thefts are open and avowed;
  And I confess them, which you dare not.
Sausage-seller. But I can take false oaths aloud,
  And in the presence of a crowd;
   And if they know the fact I care not.
Cleon. What! do you venture to invade
  My proper calling and my trade?
  But I denounce here, on the spot,
  The sacrificial tripe you've got;
   The tithe it owes was never paid:
  It owes a tithe, I say, to Jove;
  You've wronged and robbed the powers above.

Chorus. Dark and unsearchably profound abyss,
    Gulf of unfathomable
    Baseness and iniquity!
    Miracle of immense,
    Intense impudence!
    Every court, every hall,
    Juries and assemblies, all
    Are stunned to death, deafened all,
    Whilst you bawl,
    The bench and bar
    Ring and jar.
    Each decree
    Smells of thee,
    Land and sea
    Stink of thee.
       Whilst we
Scorn and hate, execrate, abominate,
Thee the brawler and embroiler of the nation and the
   State.
  You that on the rocky seat of our assembly raise a din,

Deafening all our ears with uproar, as you rave and howl
and grin;
Watching all the while the vessels with revenue sailing in.
Like the tunny-fishers perched aloft, to look about and
bawl,
When the shoals are seen arriving, ready to secure a haul.

Cleon. I was aware of this affair, and every stitch of it I know,
Where the plot was cobbled up and patched together, long
ago.

Sausage-seller. Cobbling is your own profession, tripe and
sausages are mine:
But the country folks complain, that in a fraudulent design,
You retailed them skins of treaties, that appeared like
trusty leather,
Of a peace secure and lasting; but the wear-and-tear and
weather
Proved it all decayed and rotten, only fit for sale and show.

Demosthenes. Yes! a pretty trick he served me; there was I
despatched to go,
Trudged away to Pergasae, but found upon arriving there,
That myself and my commission, both were out at heels
and bare.

Chorus.   Even in your tender years,
                    And your early disposition,
               You betrayed an inward sense
               Of the conscious impudence,
                    Which constitutes a politician.

Hence you squeeze and drain alone the rich milch kine of
our allies;
Whilst the son of Hippodamus licks his lips with longing eyes.
          But now, with eager rapture we behold
          A mighty miscreant of baser mould!
          A more consummate ruffian!

An energetic ardent ragamuffin!
Behold him there! He stands before your eyes,
To bear you down, with a superior frown,
        A fiercer stare,
And more incessant and exhaustless lies.

[To the Sausage-seller.]

Now then do you, that boast a birth, from whence you might
        inherit,
And from your breeding have derived a manhood and a spirit,
Unbroken by the rules of art, untamed by education,
Show forth the native impudence and vigour of the nation!
Sausage-seller. Well; if you like, then, I'll describe the nature
        of him clearly,
    The kind of rogue I've known him for.
Cleon.   My friend, you're somewhat early.
    First give *me* leave to speak.
Sausage-seller.   I won't, by Jove! Aye. You may bellow!
    I'll make you know, before I go, that I'm the baser fellow.
Chorus. Aye! stand to that! Stick to the point; and for a
        ·   further glory,
    Say that your family were base, time out of mind before ye.
Cleon. Let me speak first!
Sausage-seller.   I won't.
Cleon.   You shall, by Jove!
Sausage-seller.   I won't, by Jove, though!
Cleon. By Jupiter, I shall burst with rage!
Sausage-seller.   No matter, I'll prevent you.
Chorus. No; don't prevent, for Heaven's sake! Don't hinder
        him from bursting.
Cleon. What means—what ground of hope have you—to
        dare to speak against me?
Sausage-seller. What! I can speak! and I can chop—garlic
        and lard and logic.

Cleon. Aye! You're a speaker, I suppose! I should enjoy to
see you,
Like a pert scullion set to cook—to see your talents fairly
Put to the test, with hot blood-raw disjointed news arriving,
Obliged to hash and season it, and dish it in an instant.
You're like the rest of 'em—the swarm of paltry weak
pretenders.
You've made your pretty speech perhaps, and gained a
little lawsuit
Against a merchant foreigner, by dint of water-drinking,
And lying long awake o' nights, composing and repeating,
And studying as you walked the streets, and wearing out
the patience
Of all your friends and intimates, with practising before-
hand:
And now you wonder at yourself, elated and delighted
At your own talent for debate—you silly saucy coxcomb.
Sausage-seller. What's your own diet? How do you contrive
to keep the city
Passive and hushed—What kind of drink drives ye to that
presumption?
Cleon. Why mention any man besides, that's capable to match
me;
That after a sound hearty meal of tunny-fish and cutlets,
Can quaff my gallon; and at once, without premeditation,
With slang and jabber overpower the generals at Pylos?
Sausage-seller. But I can eat my paunch of pork, my liver
and my haslets,
And scoop the sauce with both my hands; and with my
dirty fingers
I'll seize old Nicias by the throat, and choke the grand
debaters.
Chorus. We like your scheme in some respects; but still that
style of feeding,

Keeping the sauce all to yourself, appears a gross
    proceeding.
Cleon. But I can domineer and dine on mullets at Miletus.
Sausage-seller. And I can eat my shins of beef, and farm the
    mines of silver.
Cleon. I'll burst into the Council House, and storm and blow
    and bluster.
Sausage-seller. I'll blow the wind into your tail, and kick you
    like a bladder.
Cleon. I'll tie you neck and heels at once, and kick ye to the
    kennel.
Chorus. Begin with us then! Try your skill!—kicking us
    all together!
Cleon. I'll have ye pilloried in a trice.
Sausage-seller. I'll have you tried for cowardice.
Cleon. I'll tan your hide to cover seats.
Sausage-seller. Yours shall be made a purse for cheats.
    The luckiest skin that could be found.
Cleon. Dog, I'll pin you to the ground
    With ten thousand tenter-hooks.
Sausage-seller. I'll equip you for the cooks,
    Neatly prepared, with skewers and lard.
Cleon. I'll pluck your eyebrows off, I will.
Sausage-seller. I'll cut your collops out, I will.

The Oracle-Mongers

THE KNIGHTS 997–1110.

*Re-enter Cleon and the Sausage-seller—Cleon with a large
    packet and the Sausage-seller staggering under a porter's
    load.*

Cleon [*to Demus*]. Well, there a bundle you see, I've brought
    of 'em;
    But that's not all; there's more of them to come—

Sausage-seller. I grunt and sweat, you see, with the load
  of 'em;
 But that's not all; there's more of 'em to come.
Demus. But what are these?—all?
Cleon.   Oracles.
Demus.   What, all?
Cleon. Ah, you're surprised, it seems, at the quantity!
 That's nothing; I've a trunk full of 'em at home.
Sausage-seller. And I've a garret and out-house both brimful.
Demus. Let's give 'em a look. Whose oracles are these?
Cleon. Bakis's mine are.
Demus [*to the Sausage-seller*]. Well, and whose are yours?
Sausage-seller. Mine are from Glanis, Bakis's elder brother.
Demus. And what are they all about?
Cleon.   About the Athenians,
 About the Island of Pylos—about myself—
 About yourself—about all kinds of things.
Demus. And what are yours about?
Sausage-seller.   About the Athenians—
 About pease-pudding, and porridge—about the Spartans—
 About the war—about the pilchard fishery—
 About the state of things in general—
 About short weights and measures in the market—
 About all things and persons whatsoever—
 About yourself and me. Bid him go whistle.
Demus. Come, read them out then! that one in particular,
 My favourite one of all, about the eagle;
 About my being an eagle in the clouds.
Cleon. Listen then! Give your attention to the Oracle!
 "Son of Erechtheus, mark and ponder well,
 This holy warning from Apollo's cell.
 It bids thee cherish him, the sacred whelp,
 Who for thy sake doth bite and bark and yelp.
 Guard and protect him from the chattering jay;
F

So shall thy juries all be kept in pay."

Demus. That's quite above me! Erechtheus and a whelp!
   What should Erechtheus do with a whelp or a jay?
   What does it mean?

Cleon.   The meaning of it is this:
   I am presignified as a dog, who barks
   And watches for you. Apollo therefore bids you
   Cherish the sacred whelp—meaning myself.

Sausage-seller. I tell ye, the Oracle means no such thing:
   This whelp has gnawed the corner off; but here,
   I've a true perfect copy.

Demus.   Read it out then!
   Meanwhile I'll pick a stone up for the nonce,
   For fear the dog in the Oracle should bite me.

Sausage-seller. "Son of Erechtheus, 'ware the gap-toothed
               dog,
   The crafty mongrel that purloins thy prog;
   Fawning at meals, and filching scraps away,
   The whilst you gape and stare another way;
   He prowls by night, and pilfers many a prize,
   Amidst the sculleries and the colonies."

Demus. Well, Glanis has the best of it, I declare.

Cleon. First listen, my good friend, and then decide:
   "In sacred Athens shall a woman dwell,
   Who shall bring forth a lion fierce and fell;
   This lion shall defeat the gnats and flies,
   Which are that noble nation's enemies.
   Him you must guard and keep for public good,
   With iron bulwarks and a wall of wood."

Demus [*to the Sausage-seller*]. D'ye understand it?

Sausage-seller.   No, not I, by Jove!

Cleon. Apollo admonishes you to guard and keep me;
   I am the lion here alluded to.

Demus. A lion! Why, just now you were a dog!

Sausage-seller. Aye, but he stifles the true sense of it,
  Designedly—that "wooden and iron wall"
  In which Apollo tells ye he should be kept.
Demus. What did the deity mean by it? What d'ye think?
Sausage-seller. To have him kept in the pillory and the stocks.
Demus. That prophecy seems likely to be verified.
Cleon. "Heed not their strain; for crows and daws abound,
  But love your faithful hawk, victorious found,
  Who brought the Spartan magpies tied and bound."
Sausage-seller. "The Paphlagonian, impudent and rash,
  Risked that adventure in a drunken dash.
  O simple son of Cecrops, ill advised!
  I see desert in arms unfairly prized:
  Men only can secure and kill the game;
  A woman's deed it is to cook the same."
Cleon. Do listen at least to the Oracle about Pylos:
  "Pylos there is behind, and eke before,
  The bloody Pylos."
Demus.   Let me hear no more!
  Those Pylos's are my torment evermore.
Sausage-seller. But here's an Oracle which you must attend
          to;
  About the navy—a very particular one.
Demus. Yes, I'll attend—I wish it would tell me how
  To pay my seamen their arrears of wages.
Sausage-seller. "O son of Egeus, ponder and beware
  Of the dog-fox, so crafty, lean, and spare,
  Subtle and swift." Do ye understand it?
Demus.   Yes!
  Of course the dog-fox means Philostratus.
Sausage-seller. That's not the meaning—but the Paphlagonian
  Is always urging you to send out ships;
  Cruising about exacting contributions;
  A thing that Apollo positively forbids.

Demus. But why are the ships here called dog-foxes?
Sausage-seller.   Why?
   Because the ships are swift, and dogs are swift.
Demus. But what has a fox to do with it? Why dog-foxes?
Sausage-seller. The fox is a type of the ship's crew; marauding
   And eating up the vineyards.
Demus.   Well, so be it!
   But how are my foxes to get paid their wages?
Sausage-seller. I'll settle it all, and make provision for them,
   Three days' provision, presently. Only now,
   This instant, let me remind you of an Oracle:
   "Beware Cullene."
Demus.   What's the meaning of it?
Sausage-seller. Cullene, in the sense I understand,
   Implies a kind of a *culling*, asking hand—
   The *coiled* hand of an informing bully,
   Culling a bribe from his affrighted *cully*,
   A hand like this.
Cleon.   No, no! you're quite mistaken,
   It alludes to Diopithes's lame hand.
   "But here's a glorious prophecy which sings,
   How you shall rule on earth, and rank with kings,
   And soar aloft in air on eagle's wings."
Sausage-seller. "And some of mine foretell that you shall be
   Sovereign of all the world and the Red Sea;
   And sit on juries in Ecbatana,
   Munching sweet buns and biscuit all the day."
Cleon. "But me Minerva loves, and I can tell
   Of a portentous vision that befell—
   The goddess in my sleep appeared to me,
   Holding a flagon, as it seemed to be,
   From which she poured upon the old man's crown
   Wealth, health, and peace, like ointment running down."
Sausage-seller. "And I too dreamt a dream, and it was this:

Minerva came from the Acropolis,
There came likewise, her serpent and her owl;
And in her hand she held a certain bowl;
And poured ambrosia on the old man's head,
And salt-fish pickle upon yours instead."
Demus. Well, Glanis is the cleverest after all.
And therefore I'm resolved, from this time forth,
To put myself into your charge and keeping;
To be tended in my old age and taken care of.
Cleon. No, do pray wait a little; and see how regularly
I'll furnish you with a daily dole of barley.
Demus. Don't tell me of barley! I can't bear to hear of it!
I've been cajoled and choused more than enough
By Thouphanes and yourself this long time past.
Cleon. Then I'll provide you delicate wheaten flour.
Sausage-seller. And I'll provide you manchets, and roast meat,
And messes piping hot that cry "Come eat me."
Demus. Make haste then, both of ye. Whatever you do—
And whichever of the two befriends me most,
I'll give him up the management of the State.
Cleon. Well, I'll be first then.
Sausage-seller.   No, you sha'n't, 'tis I.
[*Both run off; but the Sausage-seller contrives to get
the start.*]

"*Feed the Brute*"

THE FROGS 503–578.

*Enter Proserpine's Servant Maid (a kind of Dame Quickly),
who immediately addresses Xanthias.*

Dear Hercules. Well, you're come at last. Come in,
For the goddess, as soon as she heard of it, set to work
Baking peck loaves, and frying stacks of pancakes,
And making messes of furmety; there's an ox

Besides, she has roasted whole, with a relishing stuffing,
  If you'll only just step in this way.
Xanthias [*with dignity and reserve*]. I thank you,
  I'm equally obliged.
Servant Maid.   No, no, by Jupiter!
  We must not let you off, indeed. There's wild fowl,
  And sweetmeats for the dessert, and the best of wine;
  Only walk in.
Xanthias [*as before*]. I thank you. You'll excuse me.
Servant Maid. No, no, we can't excuse you, indeed we can't;
  There are dancing and singing girls besides.
Xanthias [*with dissembled emotion*].   What! dancers?
Servant Maid. Yes, that there are; the sweetest, charmingest
        things
  That you ever saw—and there's the cook this moment
  Is dishing up the dinner.
Xanthias [*with an air of lofty condescension*]. Go before then,
  And tell the girls—those singing girls you mention'd—
  To prepare for my approach in person presently.
      [*To Bacchus.*] You, sirrah! follow behind me with the
        bundles.
Bacchus. Holloh, you! what, do you take the thing in earnest,
  Because, for a joke, I drest you up like Hercules?
          [*Xanthias continues to gesticulate as Hercules.*
  Come, don't stand fooling, Xanthias. You'll provoke me.
  There, carry the bundles, sirrah, when I bid you.
Xanthias [*relapsing at once into his natural air*].
  Why, sure, do you mean to take the things away
  That you gave me yourself of your own accord this instant?
Bacchus. I never mean a thing; I do it at once.
  Let go of the lion's skin directly, I tell you.
Xanthias [*resigning his heroical insignia with a tragical air
        and tone*].
  To you, just Gods, I make my last appeal,

Bear witness!

Bacchus. What! the Gods?—do you think they mind you?
How could you take it in your head, I wonder;
Such a foolish fancy for a fellow like you,
A mortal and a slave, to pass for Hercules?

Xanthias. There. Take them.—There—you may have
them—but, please God,
You may come to want my help some time or other.

Chorus.   Dexterous and wily wits
          Find their own advantage ever;
      For the wind, where'er it sits,
          Leaves a berth secure and clever
      To the ready navigator;
      That foresees and knows the nature
      Of the wind and weather's drift;
      And betimes can turn and shift
      To the shelter'd easy side;
      'Tis a practice proved and tried,
      Not to wear a formal face;
      Fixt in attitude and place,
      Like an image on its base;
      'Tis the custom of the seas,
      Which, as all the world agrees,
      Justifies Theramenes.

Bacchus.   How ridiculous and strange;
          What a monstrous proposition,
      That I should condescend to change
          My dress, my name, and my condition,
      To follow Xanthias, and behave
      Like a mortal and a slave;
      To be set to watch the door
      While he wallow'd with his whore,

Tumbling on a purple bed;
While I waited with submission,
To receive a broken head;
Or be kick'd upon suspicion
Of impertinence and peeping
At the joys that he was reaping.

As Bacchus was before made answerable for the offence which
Hercules had committed in seizing Cerberus, he is now accused of
other misdemeanours which Hercules (agreeably to the character
of voracity and violence which was attributed to him by the comic
writers) might be supposed to have committed in the course of the
same expedition.

Enter Two Women, Sutlers or Keepers of an Eating-House.

1*st Woman.* What, Platana! Goody Platana! there! that's he,
The fellow that robs and cheats poor victuallers;
That came to our house and eat those nineteen loaves.
2*nd Woman.* Ay, sure enough that's he, the very man.
Xanthias [tauntingly to Bacchus]. There's mischief in the
wind for somebody!
1*st Woman.* —And a dozen and a half of cutlets and fried
chops,
At a penny halfpenny a piece—
Xanthias [significantly].   There are pains and penalties
Impending—
1*st Woman.*   —And all the garlic: such a quantity
As he swallow'd—
*Bacchus [delivers this speech with Herculean dignity, after his
fashion; having hitherto remained silent upon the same
principle].*   Woman, you're beside yourself;
You talk you know not what—
2*nd Woman.*   No, no! you reckon'd
I should not know you again with them there buskins.
1*st Woman.* —Good lack! and there was all that fish besides.
Indeed—with the pickle, and all—and the good green
cheese

That he gorged at once, with the rind, and the rush-baskets,
And then, when I call'd for payment, he look'd fierce,
And stared at me in the face, and grinn'd, and roar'd—
Xanthias. Just like him! That's the way wherever he goes.
1*st Woman.*   —And snatch'd his sword out, and behaved
    like mad.
Xanthias. Poor souls! you suffer'd sadly!
1*st Woman.*   Yes, indeed;
And then we both ran off with the fright and terror,
And scrambled into the loft beneath the roof;
And he took up two rugs and stole them off.
Xanthias. Just like him again—
1*st Woman.*   But something must be done.
    Go call me Cleon, he's my advocate.
2*nd Woman.* And Hyperbolus, if you meet him send him here.
    He's mine; and we'll demolish him, I warrant.
1*st Woman* [*going close up to Bacchus, in the true termagant
    attitude of rage and defiance, with the arms akimbo, and
    a neck and chin thrust out*].
    How I should like to strike those ugly teeth out
    With a good big stone, you ravenous greedy villain!
    You gormandising villain! that I should—
    Yes, that I should; your wicked ugly fangs
    That have eaten up my substance, and devour'd me.
2*nd Woman.* And I could toss you into the public pit
    With the malefactors' carcases; that I could,
    With pleasure and satisfaction; that I could.
1*st Woman.* And I should like to rip that gullet out
    With a reaping hook, that swallow'd all my tripe,
    And liver and lights—but I'll fetch Cleon here,
    And he shall summon him. He shall settle him,
    And have it out of him this very day.
                [*Exeunt* 1*st and* 2*nd Woman.*

Trial by Torture

THE FROGS 605–673.

Aeacus. Arrest me there that fellow that stole my dog.
  There!—Pinion him!—Quick!
Bacchus [*tauntingly to Xanthias*]. There's somebody in a
    scrape.
Xanthias [*in a menacing attitude*]. Keep off, and be hang'd.
Aeacus.   Oh, hoh! do you mean to fight for it?
  Here! Pardokas, and Skeblias, and the rest of ye,
  Make up to the rogue, and settle him. Come, be quick.
    [*A scuffle ensues, in which Xanthias succeeds in obliging
      Aeacus's runners to keep their distance.*]
Bacchus [*mortified at Xanthias's prowess*].
  Well, is not this quite monstrous and outrageous,
  To steal the dog, and then to make an assault
  In justification of it?
Xanthias [*triumphantly and ironically*]. Quite outrageous!
Aeacus [*gravely, and dissembling his mortification*].
  An aggravated case!
Xanthias [*with candour and gallantry*]. Well, now—by
        Jupiter,
  May I die, but I never saw this place before—
  Nor ever stole the amount of a farthing from you:
  Nor a hair of your dog's tail.—But you shall see now,
  I'll settle all this business nobly and fairly.
  —This slave of mine—you may take and torture him;
  And if you make out any thing against me,
  You may take and put me to death for aught I care.
Aeacus [*in an obliging tone, softened into deference and civility
    by the liberality of Xanthias's proposal*].
  But which way would you please to have him tortured?
Xanthias [*with a gentlemanly spirit of accommodation*].
  In your own way—with . . . the lash—with . . . knots and
    screws,

With . . . the common usual customary tortures—
With the rack—with . . . the water-torture—any way—
With fire and vinegar—all sorts of ways.
[*After a very slight pause.*] There's only one thing I should
    warn you of:
I must not have him treated like a child,
To be whipt with fennel, or with lettuce leaves.

Aeacus. That's fair—and if so be . . . he's maim'd or crippled
In any respect—the valy shall be paid you.

Xanthias. Oh no!—by no means! not to me!—by no means!
You must not mention it!—Take him to the torture.

Aeacus. It had better be here, and under your own eye.
    [*To Bacchus.*] Come, you—put down your bundles and
        make ready.
And mind—Let me hear no lies!

Bacchus.   I'll tell you what:
I'd advise people not to torture me;
I give you notice—I'm a deity.
So mind now—you'll have nobody to blame
But your own self—

Aeacus.   What's that you're saying there?

Bacchus. Why, that I'm Bacchus, Jupiter's own son:
    That fellow there's a slave.   [*Pointing to Xanthias.*

Aeacus [*to Xanthias*].   Do ye hear?

Xanthias.   I hear him—
A reason the more to give him a good beating;
If he's immortal he need never mind it.

Bacchus. Why should not you be beat as well as I then,
If you're immortal, as you say you are?

Xanthias. Agreed—and him, the first that you see flinching,
Or seeming to mind it at all, you may set him down
For an impostor and no real deity.

Aeacus [*to Xanthias, with warmth and cordiality*].
    Ah, you're a worthy gentleman, I'll be bound for't;

You're all for the truth and the proof. Come—strip there,
    both o' ye.
Xanthias. But how can ye put us to the question fairly,
    Upon equal terms?
Aeacus [*in the tone of a person proposing a convenient, agree-*
    able arrangement]. Oh, easily enough,
    Conveniently enough—a lash apiece,
    Each in your turn: you can have 'em one by one.
Xanthias. That's right. [*Putting himself in an attitude to*
    receive the blow.]
                Now mind if ye see me flinch or swerve.
Aeacus [*strikes him, but without producing any expression of*
    pain].
    I've struck.
Xanthias.   Not you!
Aeacus.   Why it seems as if I had not.
    I'll smite this other fellow.   [*Strikes Bacchus.*
Bacchus [*pretending not to feel*]. When will you do it?

Aeacus perseveres and applies his discipline alternately to Bacchus
and Xanthias, and extorts from them various involuntary exclama-
tions of pain, which they immediately account for and justify in
some ridiculous way. The passage cannot be translated literally,
but an idea may be given of it. Suppose Bacchus to receive a blow,
he exclaims—

Oh dear! [*and immediately subjoins*] companions of my
    youthful years.
Xanthias [*to Aeacus*]. Did ye hear? he made an outcry.
Aeacus.   What was that?
Bacchus. A favourite passage from Archilochus.
    [*Xanthias receives a blow, and exclaims*]
    O Jupiter! [*and subjoins*] that on the Idean height.
    [*And contends that he has been repeating the first line*
        of a well-known hymn. Aeacus at length gives the
        matter up.]
Well, after all my pains, I'm quite at a loss

To discover which is the true, real deity.
By the Holy Goddess—I'm completely puzzled;
I must take you before Proserpine and Pluto;
Being gods themselves they're likeliest to know.
Bacchus. Why, that's a lucky thought. I only wish
It had happen'd to occur before you beat us.

The New City

THE BIRDS 1118–1693.

Peisthetairus. Well, friends and birds! the sacrifice has
    succeeded,
Our omens have been good ones: good and fair.
But, what's the meaning of it? We've no news
From the new building yet! No messenger!
Oh! there, at last, I see—there's somebody
Running at speed, and panting like a racer.

*Enter a Messenger, quite out of breath; and speaking in
short snatches.*

Messenger. Where is he? Where? Where is he? Where?
    Where is he?—
The president Peisthetairus?
Peisthetairus [*coolly*].   Here am I.
Messenger [*in a gasp of breath*]. Your fortification's finished.
Peisthetairus.   Well! that's well.
Messenger. A most amazing, astonishing work it is!
So, that Theagenes and Proxenides
Might flourish and gasconade and prance away,
Quite at their ease, both of them four-in-hand,
Driving abreast upon the breadth of the wall,
Each in his own new chariot.
Peisthetairus.   You surprise me.

Messenger. And the height (for I made the measurement
        myself)
  Is exactly a hundred fathoms.
Peisthetairus.   Heaven and earth!
  How could it be? such a mass! Who could have built it?
Messenger. The Birds; no creature else, no foreigners,
  Egyptian bricklayers, workmen or masons,
  But, they themselves, alone, by their own efforts
  (Even to my surprise, as an eye-witness)—
  The Birds, I say, completed everything:
    There came a body of thirty thousand cranes
  (I won't be positive, there might be more)
  With stones from Africa, in their craws and gizzards,
  Which the stone-curlews and stone-chatterers
  Worked into shape and finished. The sand-martins
  And mud-larks, too, were busy in their department,
  Mixing the mortar, while the water birds,
  As fast as it was wanted, brought the water
  To temper, and work it.
Peisthetairus [*in a fidget*].   But, who served the masons?
  Who did you get to carry it?
Messenger.   To carry it?
  Of course, the carrion crows and carrying pigeons.
Peisthetairus [*in a fuss, which he endeavours to conceal*]
  Yes! yes! But after all, to load your hods,
  How did you manage that?
Messenger.   Oh, capitally,
  I promise you. There were the geese, all barefoot,
  Trampling the mortar, and, when all was ready,
  They handed it into the hods, so cleverly,
  With their flat feet!
Peisthetairus. [*A bad joke, as a vent for irritation.*]
                They *footed* it, you mean—
  Come; it was handily done though, I confess.

Messenger. Indeed, I assure you, it was a sight to see them;
  And trains of ducks there were, clambering the ladders,
  With their duck legs, like bricklayers' 'prentices,
  All dapper and handy, with their little trowels.
Peisthetairus. In fact, then, it's no use engaging foreigners,
  Mere folly and waste, we've all within ourselves.
    Ah, well now, come! But about the woodwork? Heh!
  Who were the carpenters? Answer me that!
Messenger. The woodpeckers, of course; and there they were,
  Labouring upon the gates, driving and banging,
  With their hard hatchet beaks, and such a din,
  Such a clatter, as they made, hammering and hacking,
  In a perpetual peal, pelting away
  Like shipwrights, hard at work in the arsenal.
    And now their work is finished, gates and all,
  Staples and bolts, and bars and everything;
  The sentries at their posts; patrols appointed;
  The watchmen in the barbican; the beacons
  Ready prepared for lighting; all their signals
  Arranged—but I'll step out, just for a moment,
  To wash my hands. You'll settle all the rest.   [*Exit.*
    [*Peisthetairus, surprised at the rapid conclusion of the
      work, feeling from the volubility and easy manner of
      the Messenger the blow which his authority has
      received; seeing that nothing is left for him to super-
      intend, nothing to direct, nothing to suggest, or to find
      fault with, remains in an attitude of perplexity and
      astonishment, with his hands clasped across his
      forehead.*]
Chorus [*to Peisthetairus, in a sort of self-satisfied drawling tone*].
  Heigh-day! Why, what's the matter with ye? Sure!
  Ah! well now, I calculate, you're quite astonished;
  You did not know the nature of our birds:
  I guess you thought it an impossible thing,

To finish up your fortification job
Within the time so cleverly.
Peisthetairus [*recovering himself and looking round*]. Yes, truly,
   Yes, I'm surprised indeed; I must confess—
     I could almost imagine to myself
   It was a dream, an illusion, altogether—
     But, there's the watchman of the town, I see!
   In alarm and haste, it seems! He's running here—

    The Watchman enters, with a shout of alarm.

—Well, what's the matter?
Watchman.   A most dreadful business:
   One of the gods, just now—Jupiter's gods—
   Has bolted through the gates, and driven on
   Right into the atmosphere, in spite of us,
   And all the jackdaws, that were mounting guard.
Peisthetairus [*animated at the prospect of having something to
     manage*].
   What an outrage! what an insult! Which of 'em?
   Which of the gods?
Watchman.   We can't pretend to say;
   We just could ascertain that he wore wings.
   We're clear upon that point.
Peisthetairus.   But a light party
   Ought surely to have been sent in such a case;
   A detachment—
Watchman.   A detachment has been sent
   Already: a squadron of ten thousand hawks,
   Besides a corps of twenty thousand hobby hawks,
   As a light cavalry, to scour the country:
   Vultures and falcons, ospreys, eagles, all
   Have sallied forth; the sound of wings is heard,
   Rushing and whizzing round on every side,
   In eager search. The fugitive divinity

Is not far off, and soon must be discovered.
Peisthetairus. Did nobody think of slingers? Where are they?
Where are the slingers got to? Give me a sling.
Arrows and slings, I say!—Make haste with 'em.

The verses which follow belong to a species of songs which are
alluded to in Aristophanes more than once. They may properly
be called "Watch-songs," being sung by the Watchmen and Soldiers
on guard, to keep themselves and their comrades awake and alert.

Chorus.   War is at hand,
                 On air and land,
                    Proclaimed and fixt.
                 War and strife,
                 Eager and rife,
                    Are kindled atwixt
                 This State of ours,
                 And the heavenly powers.
                    Look with care
                 To the circuit of air,
                    Watch lest he,
                    The deity,
                 Whatever he be,
                    Should unaware
                 Escape and flee.

But hark! the rushing sound of hasty wings
Approaches us. The deity is at hand.
Peisthetairus. Holloh, you! Where are ye flying? Where are
                 ye going?
Hold! Halt! Stop there, I tell ye!—Stop this instant!
What are ye? Where do you come from? Speak, explain.
Iris. Me? From the gods, to be sure! the Olympian gods.
Peisthetairus [*pointing to the flaunting appendages of her dress*].
What are ye? With all your flying trumpery!
A helmet? or a galley? What's your name?
   G

Iris. Iris, the messenger of the gods.

Peisthetairus. A messenger!

Oh! you're a naval messenger, I reckon.

The Salaminian galley, or the Paralian?

You're in full sail, I see.

Iris. What's here to do?

Peisthetairus. Are there no birds in waiting? Nobody

To take her into custody?

Iris. Me to custody?

Why, what's all this?

Peisthetairus. You'll find to your cost, I promise ye.

Iris. Well, this seems quite unaccountable!

Peisthetairus. Which of the gates

Did ye enter at, ye jade? How came you here?

Iris. Gates!—I know nothing about your gates, not I.

Peisthetairus. Fine innocent ignorant airs she gives herself!

You applied to the pelicans, I suppose?—The captain

Of the cormorants on guard admitted you?

Iris. Why, what the plague! what's this?

Peisthetairus. So, you confess!

You come without permission!

Iris. Are you mad?

Peisthetairus. Did neither the sitting magistrates nor bird-
masters

Examine and pass you?

Iris. Examine me, forsooth!

Peisthetairus. This is the way then!—without thanks or leave

You ramble and fly, committing trespasses

In an atmosphere belonging to your neighbours!

Iris. And where would you have us fly then? Us, the gods!

Peisthetairus. I neither know nor care. But, I know this,

They sha'n't fly here. And another thing I know.

I know—that, if there ever was an instance

Of an Iris or a rainbow, such as you,

Detected in the fact, fairly condemned,
And justly put to death—it would be you.
Iris. But, I'm immortal!
Peisthetairus [*coolly and peremptorily*]. That would make no
   difference:
We should be strangely circumstanced indeed;
With the possession of a sovereign power,
And you, the gods, in no subordination,
No kind of order! fairly mutinying,
Infringing and disputing our commands.
—Now then, you'll please to tell me—where you're going?
Which way you're steering with those wings of yours?
Iris. I? . . . I'm commissioned from my father Jove,
 To summon human mortals to perform
 Their rites and offerings and oblations, due
 To the powers above.
Peisthetairus.   And who do you mean? what powers?
Iris. What powers? Ourselves, the Olympian deities!
Peisthetairus. So then! you're deities, the rest of ye!
Iris. Yes, to be sure What others should there be?
Peisthetairus. Remember!—once for all!—that we, the
   Birds,
Are the only deities, from this time forth;
And not your father Jove. By Jove! not he!
Iris. Oh! rash, presumptuous wretch! Incense no more
 The wrath of the angry gods! lest ruin drive
 Her ploughshare o'er thy mansion; and destruction,
 With hasty besom, sweep thee to the dust;
 Or flaming lightning smite thee with a flash,
 Left in an instant smouldering and extinct.
Peisthetairus. Do ye hear her?—Quite in tragedy!—quite
   sublime!
Come, let me try for a bouncer in return.
Let's see. Let's recollect. "Me dost thou deem,

Like a base Lydian or a Phrygian slave,
With hyperbolical bombast to scare?"
I tell ye, and you may tell him: Jupiter—
If he provokes me, and pushes things too far—
Will see some eagles of mine, to outnumber his,
With firebrands in their claws about his house.
  And, I shall send a flight of my Porphyrions,
A hundred covey or more, armed cap-à-pie,
To assault him in his sublime celestial towers:
Perhaps, he may remember in old times,
He found enough to do with one Porphyrion.
  And for you, Madam Iris, I shall strip
Your rainbow-shanks, if you're impertinent,
Depend upon it, and I myself, in person,
Will ruin you, myself!—Old as I am.

Iris. Curse ye, you wretch, and all your filthy words.

Peisthetairus. Come, scuttle away; convey your person else-
      where;
Be brisk, and leave a vacancy. Brush off.

Iris. I shall inform my father. He shall know
Your rudeness and impertinence. He shall,—
He'll settle ye and keep ye in order. You shall see.

Peisthetairus. Oh dear! is it come to that! No, you're mis-
      taken,
Young woman, upon that point; I'm not your man,
I'm an old fellow grown; I'm thunder-proof,
Proof against flames and darts and female arts:
You'd best look out for a younger customer.

Poor Iris, in her rage, unwittingly makes use of the same sort of
phrase with which a young girl at Athens would repel, or affect to
repel, improper familiarities. Peisthetairus, taking advantage of
this, pretends to consider her indignation as a mere coquettish
artifice intended to inveigle and allure him.
  The *Athenian Father*—"I shall inform my father"—may be
considered as equivalent to the *Irish Brother*. The menace in one
case would imply a duel, in the other a lawsuit.

Chorus. Notice is hereby given
   To the deities of heaven;
    Not to trespass here,
    Upon our atmosphere;
   Take notice; from the present day,
    No smoke or incense is allowed
    To pass this way.

Peisthetairus. Quite strange it is! quite unaccountable!
 That herald to mankind, that was despatched,
 What has become of him? He's not yet returned.

Enter Herald.

Herald. O Peisthetairus, happiest, wisest, best,
 Cleverest of men! Oh! most illustrious!
 Oh! most inordinately fortunate!
 Oh! most . . . Oh! do for shame, do, bid me have done.
Peisthetairus. What are you saying?
Herald.   All the people of Earth
 Have joined in a complimentary vote, decreeing
 A crown of gold to you, for your exertions.
Peisthetairus. I'm much obliged to the people of Earth. But
    why?
 What was their motive?
Herald.   O most noble founder
 Of this supereminent celestial city,
 You can't conceive the clamour of applause,
 The enthusiastic popularity,
 That attends upon your name; the impulse and stir,
 That moves among mankind, to colonise
 And migrate hither. In the time before,
 There was a Spartan mania, and people went
 Stalking about the streets, with Spartan staves,
 With their long hair, unwashed and slovenly,

Like so many Socrates's: but, of late,
Birds are the fashion—Birds are all in all—
Their modes of life are grown to be mere copies
Of the birds' habits; rising with the lark;
Scratching and scrabbling suits and informations;
Picking and pecking upon points of law;
Brooding and hatching evidence. In short,
It has grown to such a pitch, that names of birds
Are given to individuals; Chaerephon
Is called an owl, Theagenes a goose,
Philocles a cock sparrow, Midias
A dunghill cock. And all the songs in vogue
Have something about birds, swallows or doves;
Or about flying, or a wish for wings.
    Such is the state of things, and I must warn you,
That you may expect to see some thousands of them
Arriving here, almost immediately,
With a clamorous demand for wings and claws:
I advise you to provide yourself in time.
Peisthetairus. Come, it won't do then, to stand dawdling here:
    Go you, fill the hampers and the baskets there
    With wings, and bid the loutish porter bring them,
    While I stop here, to encounter the new-comers.

Chorus.   Shortly shall the noble town,
          Populous and gay,
      Shine in honour and renown.
Peisthetairus [*drily*].
          Why, perhaps she may.
Chorus.   The benignant powers of love,
          From their happy sphere,
      From the blest abodes above . . .
Peisthetairus [*venting his ill-humour on the servant*].
          Curse ye, rascal! can't ye move!

Chorus   . . . Are descending here.
                  Where in all this earthly range,
                  He that wishes for a change
                          Can he find a seat,
                  Joyous and secure as this,
                  Filled with happiness and bliss,
                          Such a fair retreat?
                  Here are all the lovely faces,
                  Gentle Venus and the Graces,
                          And the little Cupid;
                  Order, ease and harmony,
                  Peace and affability.
Peisthetairus. The scoundrel is so stupid;
                  Quicker, sirrah! bring it quicker!
Chorus.   Let him bring the woven wicker
                          With the winged store.
                  I, myself, in very deed,
                  With the varlet will proceed,
                          And smite him more and more;
                  Like a sluggish ass he seems,
                  Or even, as a man that dreams,
                          Therefore smite him sore.
Peisthetairus.   He's a lazy rogue, it's true.
Chorus. Now range them forth, displayed in order due,
     Feathers of every form and size and hue,
     With shrewd intent, adapting every pinion
     To the new residents of your dominion.
Peisthetairus. I vow by the hawks and eagles! I won't bear it;
     I'll beat ye, I will myself, you lazy rascal!

As a practical comment upon the anticipations of the Chorus,
and as a sample of the kind of population likely to resort to a new
colony, the first arrival is that of a young reprobate, who wishes
his father out of the way; and who conceives that the laws of the
Birds will permit him to hasten that desirable conclusion. Peisthetairus receives and attends to him, without being betrayed into any
expression of moral indignation, which would be inconsistent with

his character as a perfect politician. He merely states, as a matter of fact, some difficulties arising out of a point of law, professes a wish to serve him, as a hearty partisan, well disposed to the cause of the new colony; and finally, in an easy way, recalls to his recollection one of the precepts of his Catechism, and at the same time points out to him a mode of life suited to his situation and tastes. The young man, who is more of a wild desperate, than a confirmed villain, is struck with the suggestion, expresses a resolution to adopt it, and departs.

Enter a fellow, singing.

"Oh! for an eagle's force and might,
    Loftily to soar
Over land and sea, to light
    On a lonely shore."

Peisthetairus. Well, here's a song that's something to the
        purpose.
Young Man. Ay, ay, there's nothing like it—wings and
        flying!
    Wings are your only sort. I'm a bird-fancier.
    In the new fashion quite. I've taken a notion
    To settle and live amongst ye. I like your laws.
Peisthetairus. What laws do you mean? We've many laws
        amongst us.
Young Man. Your laws in general; but particularly
    The law that allows of beating one's own father.
Peisthetairus. Why, truly, yes! we esteem it a point of valour,
    In a chicken, if he clapperclaws the old cock.
Young Man. That was my view, feeling a wish in fact
    To throttle mine, and seize the property.
Peisthetairus. Yes, but you'd find some difficulties here,
    An obstacle insurmountable, I conceive;
    An ancient statute standing unrepealed,
    Engraved upon our old Ciconian columns.
    It says, that when a stork or a ciconia
    Has brought his lawful progeny of young storks
    To bird's estate, and enabled them to fly:

The sire shall stand entitled to a maintenance
At the son's cost and charge in his old age.
Young Man. I've managed finely it seems to mend myself!
Forced to maintain my father after all!
Peisthetairus. No, no; not quite so bad; since you're come
        here,
As a well-wisher to the establishment,
Zealous and friendly, we'll contrive to equip you
With a suit of armour, as a soldier's orphan.
And now, young man, let me suggest some notions,
Things that were taught me when a boy. "Your father?"
" Strike him not"—rather take this pair of wings;
And this cockspur; imagine you've a coxcomb
Upon your head, to serve you for a helmet;
Look out for service, and enlist yourself;
Get into a garrison; live upon your pay;
And let your father live. You're fond of fighting,
And fond of flying—take a flight to Thrace;
There you may please yourself; and fight your fill.
Young Man. By Jove, you're right. The notion's not a bad
        one.
    I'll follow it up!
Peisthetairus [*very gravely and quietly*]. You'll find it the
        best way.   [*Exit Young Man.*

Cinesias, a lame dithyrambic poet and musician, arrives in the hopes of being able to provide himself with wings, which will enable him to look after his concerns among the clouds, the great emporium for business with all persons who are embarked in the dithyrambic line. Peisthetairus amuses himself with affronting and laughing at him, but he persists in his purpose, and professes his determination to continue worrying and persevering till it is accomplished.

Enter Cinesias, singing.

"Fearless, I direct my flight
To the vast Olympian height;

Thence at random, I repair,
Wafted in the whirling air;
With an eddy, wild and strong,
Over all the fields of song."

Peisthetairus. Ah! well, Cinesias, I'm quite glad to see ye;
But, what has brought ye and all your songs and music,
Hobbling along with your old chromatic joints?

Cinesias [singing]. "Let me live, and let me sing,
Like a bird upon the wing."

Peisthetairus. No more of that; but tell us plainly in prose,
What are ye come for? what's your scheme, your object?

Cinesias. I was anxious to procure a pair of wings,
To say the truth; wishing to make a tour
Among the clouds, collecting images
And metaphors, and things of that description.

Peisthetairus. How so! do you procure 'em from the clouds?

Cinesias. Entirely! Our dithyrambic business absolutely
Depends upon them; our most approved commodities,
The dusty, misty, murky articles,
With the suitable wings and feathers, are imported
Exclusively from thence. I'll give you a sample,
A thing of my own composing. You shall judge.

Peisthetairus. But, indeed, I'd rather not.

Cinesias.   But, indeed, you must;
It's a summary view of flying, comprehending it
In all its parts, in every point of view.

Cinesias, singing.

"Ye gentle feathered tribes,
Of every plume and hue,
That, in uninhabited air,
Are hurrying here and there;
Oh! that I, like you,
Could leave this earthly level,

For a wild aerial revel:
 O'er the waste of ocean
To wander, and to dally
 With the billow's motion;
Or, in an eager sally,
 Soaring to the sky,
 To range and rove on high
With my plumy sails.
 Buffeted and baffled with the gusty gales,
 Buffeted and baffled . . ."

[While Cinesias is repeating these last lines, Peisthetairus
 comes behind him, and gives him a flap with a huge
 pair of wings.]

Cinesias. A pretty, civil joke indeed!

Peisthetairus.   What joke?
I'm only buffeting you with the plumy sails,
I thought it was what you wanted.

Cinesias.   Well, that's fine!
Pretty respect for a master such as me,
A leader of the band, that all the tribes
Are ready to fight for, to bespeak him first.

Peisthetairus. Well, we've a little unfledged chorus here,
That Leotrophides hatched, poor puny nestlings,
I'll give 'em you for scholars.

Cinesias.   Ah, laugh on!
Laugh on! but take my word for it, here I stay,
Till you provide me with a pair of wings,
Proper to circumnavigate the skies.   *[Exit Cinesias.*

Peisthetairus is represented in the following scene as a perfect
master of his art; amusing himself in angling and playing with a
stupid, impudent young scoundrel; sometimes twitching him in
with a slight jerk of his hook, and again allowing him to run out
to the full length of his line. If any one passage were to be selected
from the remains of Aristophanes as particularly illustrative of the
manner in which he delights to exhibit character, perhaps it would
be this; it is not a serious struggle for ascendency, such as he

displays elsewhere; in this instance, he shows Peisthetairus as a consummate practitioner, relinquishing and reassuming it at pleasure. But this is one of those scenes which, to be thoroughly appreciated, would require to be developed in dramatic action by a superior comedian. The mere printed page, unless we suppose the reader to bestow as much attention on it as an actor would do in studying his part, will be found to convey a very confused and inadequate notion of it.

Enter Sycophant, singing.

"Tell us who the strangers are,
Gentle swallow. Birds of air,
Party-coloured, poor and bare,
Tell us who the strangers are;
        Gentle swallow, tell me true."

Peisthetairus. Here's a fine plague broke out. See yonder
        fellow
Sauntering along this way, swaggering and singing.
Sycophant. Ho! gentle swallow! I say, my gentle swallow,
My gentle swallow! how often must I call?
Peisthetairus. Why, there it is; the prodigal in the fable
Seeking for swallows in a ragged coat.
Sycophant [*in an arrogant overbearing tone*]. Who's he, that's
        set to serve out wings? Where is he?
Peisthetairus. 'Tis I, but what do you want? You should
        explain.
Sycophant. Wings! Wings! You need not have asked me.
        Wings I want.
Peisthetairus. Do you mean to fly for flannel to Pellene?
Sycophant [*a little disconcerted at this allusion to his attire*].
No, no! But I'm employed . . . I employ myself,
In fact, among the allies and islanders;
I'm in the informing line.
Peisthetairus [*in a tone of very grave irony, which the
                Sycophant not perceiving, proceeds more fluently
                than before*].
                I wish you joy.

Sycophant. And a mover and manager for prosecutions,
  In criminal suits, and so forth, you understand me;
  So I wish to equip myself with a pair of wings,
  To whisk about, and trounce the islanders.
Peisthetairus. Would it be doing things in better form,
  To serve a summons flying, think ye?
Sycophant [*not knowing very well what to make of him*]. No,
  Not that, but just to avoid the risk of pirates,
  To return in company with a flight of cranes
  (As they do with the gravel in their gizzards),
  With a bellyful of lawsuits for my ballast.
Peisthetairus [*in a grave, primitive, and somewhat twaddling
        tone, intended to reanimate the impertinence of
        the Sycophant*].
  So, this is your employment! A young man
  Like you, to be an informer! Is it possible?
Sycophant. Why shouldn't it? I was never bred to labour.
Peisthetairus [*as before*]. But sure, there are other lawful
        occupations,
  In which a brisk young fellow, such as you,
  Might earn an honest, decent livelihood
  In credit and goodwill, without informing.
Sycophant [*thoroughly taken in, and thinking he has to deal
        with a mere silly well-meaning old man, becomes
        emphatically insolent*].
  Wings, my good fellow! wings I want—not words.
Peisthetairus [*drily*]. I'm giving you wings, already.
Sycophant [*a little puzzled and taken aback*].
                                  What, with words?
  Is that your way?
Peisthetairus [*in a tone of very grave banter*].
                          Yes, for mankind in general
  Are winged as it were, and brought to plume themselves
  In different ways by speeches and discourse.

Sycophant [*confused and puzzled*]. What, all?

Peisthetairus [*as before*]. Yes, all. I'll give you a striking
              instance:
   You must have heard, yourself, elderly people
   Sitting conversing in the barber's shop.
   And one says, "Well, Diitrephes has talked
   So much to my young man, he has brought him at last
   To plume himself in driving." And another
   Says, that his son is quite amongst the clouds,
   Grown flighty of late, with studying tragedy.

Sycophant [*with a sort of hesitating laugh*]. So, words are
              wings, you say.

Peisthetairus.   No doubt of it.
   I say it, and I repeat it; human nature
   Is marvellously raised and elevated
   By words. I was in hopes, that I might raise you,
   By words of good advice, to another sphere;
   To live in an honest calling.

Sycophant [*feeling himself bantered and beaten, but restive and*
              angry].   But I won't though.

Peisthetairus [*coolly*]. Why, what will you do?

Sycophant [*sulkily at first, but animating as he proceeds*].
              Why, I won't disgrace my family,
   My father and my grandfather before him
   Served as informers; and I'll stick to it,
   The profession. So, you'll please to hand 'em me out;
   A pair of your best wings, vulture's or hawk's,
   To fly to the Islands, with my summonses,
   And home again, to record them in the courts,
   And out again, to the Islands.

Peisthetairus [*in a tone of interest and sympathy, as if he was
              himself an amateur desirous of displaying his
             professional knowledge*].
              Yes, that's well,

I understand ye, I think; your method is,
To be beforehand with 'em? Your defendant,
You get him cast for non-appearance, heh?
Before he can arrive; and finish him
In his absence, heh?

Sycophant [*completely taken in, delighted—rubbing his hands*].

By Jove, you're up to it!

Peisthetairus. Then, whilst he's sailing here you get the start,
And fly, to pounce upon the property,
To rummage out the chattels.

Sycophant. That's the trick,
The notion of it!—I see you're up to it.
A man must whisk about, here and away,
Just like a whipping-top.

Peisthetairus. Ay, yes, you're right,
I understand you—the instance is a good one.
A whipping-top, you say. Well, by good luck
I've here a capital slashing suit of wings,
To serve ye, made of a cow-hide from Corcyra.

Sycophant. O heaven! what's there? a horsewhip?

Peisthetairus. Wings, I tell ye,
To whisk ye about, to flog ye, and make ye fly.

Sycophant. Oh dear! oh dear!

Peisthetairus. Scamper away, you scoundrel!
Vanish, you vagabond! whisk yourself off!
I'll pay ye for your practices in the courts,
Your pettifoggicorascalities.

[*Exit Sycophant.*

[*To the attendants.*]
Come bundle up the wings. Let's take 'em back.

[*Exeunt.*

Fabulous notions, respecting the unknown portions of the world,
seem to have been nearly the same (or at least of the same character)
in the time of Aristophanes as in the days of Sir John Mandeville.
The marvels of these regions, known only to the Birds, are

naturally expatiated upon by a Chorus of Birds, when released from the business of the stage and placed in immediate communication with the audience. But it will be seen, that by a strange coincidence those wonderful and remote objects have an unaccountable analogy to things and persons at Athens; as in the following instance of the enormous tree, which by the botanists was considered as belonging to the sycophantic genus; but which was vulgarly called a Cleonymus, whereas at Athens there happened to be a person precisely of the same name, "Cleonymus," equally distinguished for his size; and having the same peculiarity of being classed among the Sycophants. And what is more singular, as the Athenian Cleonymus had lost his shield in battle, it so happened that his vegetable counterpart was a deciduous tree, with leaves of a scutiform or shield-like shape, which it was also in the habit of losing.

The antistrophe is a romantic and mysterious description of a junketing public-house, which seems to have been in vogue; but from which it was not safe to return to town after dusk. Orestes, an heroic name, was also the name or the nickname of a noted robber. It was reckoned extremely dangerous to meet a demi-god after sunset.

Chorus : Strophe.

We have flown, and we have run,
Viewing marvels, many a one:
In every land beneath the sun.

But, the strangest sight to see,
Was a huge exotic tree,
Growing, without heart or pith,
Weak and sappy, like a wyth;
But, with leaves and boughs withal,
Comely, flourishing and tall.

This the learned all ascribe
To the sycophantic tribe;
But the natives there, like us,
Call it a Cleonymus.
In the spring's delightful hours,
It blossoms with rhetoric flowers;
I saw it standing in the field,
With leaves, in figure like a shield;
On the first tempestuous day,
I saw it cast those leaves away.

Antistrophe.

There lies a region out of sight,
Far within the realm of night,
Far from torch and candle light.
There in feasts of meal and wine,
Men and demigods may join,
There they banquet, and they dine,
Whilst the light of day prevails;
At sunset, their assurance fails.
If any mortal then presumes,
Orestes, sallying from the tombs,
Like a fierce heroic sprite,
Assaults and strips the lonely wight.

The scene which follows may be considered as a short abstract of the mode in which clandestine political information is received, attended to, and dismissed. The informant presents himself with an extraordinary display of precaution and apprehension; he is received with eagerness and cordiality, attended to with great earnestness, interrupted only by some little ill-humour on the part of the man of business, when, in seeking for information, he is obliged to betray the want of it; finally, he is dismissed with a sort of indifference, approaching to derision, after having been thoroughly pumped and drained of his intelligence.

PROMETHEUS, PEISTHETAIRUS, CHORUS

Prometheus [*enters muffled up, peeping about him with a look of anxiety and suspicion*].
　　Oh dear! If Jupiter should chance to see me!
　　Where's Peisthetairus? Where?
Peisthetairus.　　　　　　　　　　Why, what's all this?
　　This fellow muffled up?
Prometheus.　　　　　　　Do look behind me;
　　Is anybody watching? any gods
　　Following and spying after me?
Peisthetairus.　　　　　　　　　　No, none,
　　None that I can see, there's nobody. But you!
　　H

What are ye?

Prometheus.   Tell me, what's the time of day?

Peisthetairus. Why, noon, past noon; but tell me, who are ye?
     Speak.

Prometheus. Much past,—how much?

Peisthetairus [*aside*].   Confound the fool, I say!
     The insufferable blockhead!

Prometheus.   How's the sky?
     Open or overcast? Are there any clouds?

Peisthetairus [*aloud and angrily*]. Be hanged!

Prometheus.   Then I'll disguise myself no longer.

Peisthetairus. My dear Prometheus!

Prometheus.   Hold your tongue, I beg;
     Don't mention my name! If Jupiter should see me,
     Or overhear ye, I'm ruined and undone.
     But now, to give you a full complete account
     Of everything that's passing, there in heaven—
     The present state of things. . . . But first I'll trouble you
     To take the umbrella, and hold it overhead,
     Lest they should overlook us.

Peisthetairus.   What a thought!
     Just like yourself! A true Promethean thought!
     Stand under it, here! Speak boldly; never fear.

Prometheus. D'ye mind me?

Peisthetairus.   Yes, I mind ye. Speak away.

Prometheus [*emphatically*]. Jupiter's ruined.

Peisthetairus.   Ruined! How? Since when?

Prometheus. From the first hour you fortified and planted
     Your atmospheric settlements. Ever since,
     There's not a mortal offers anything
     In the shape of sacrifice. No smoke of victims!
     No fumes of incense! Absolutely nothing!
     We're keeping a strict fast—fasting perforce,
     From day to day—the whole community.

And the inland barbarous gods in the upper country
Are broken out, quite mutinous and savage,
With hunger and anger; threatening to come down
With all their force, if Jupiter refuses
To open the ports, and allow them a free traffic
For their entrails and intestines, as before.

Peisthetairus [*a little annoyed at being obliged to ask the
question*].
What—are there other barbarous gods, besides,
In the upper country?

Prometheus.   Barbarous?—to be sure!
They're all of Execestides's kindred.

Peisthetairus [*as before hesitating, but with a sort of affected
ease*].
Well—but—the name now. The same barbarous deities—
What name do you call 'em?

Prometheus [*surprised at Peisthetairus's ignorance*].
                                   Call them! The Triballi!

Peisthetairus [*giving vent to his irritation by a forced joke*].
Ah! well then, that accounts for our old saying:
Confound the *Tribe* of them!

Prometheus [*annoyed and drily*]. Precisely so.
But, now to business. Thus much I can tell ye;
That envoys will arrive immediately
From Jupiter, and those upland wild Triballi,
To treat for a peace. But, you must not consent
To ratify or conclude, till Jupiter
Acknowledges the sovereignty of the birds;
Surrendering up to you the sovereign queen,
Whom you must marry.

Peisthetairus.   Why, what queen is that?

Prometheus. What queen? A most delightful charming girl,
Jove's housekeeper, that manages his matters,
Serves out his thunderbolts, arranges everything;

The constitutional laws and liberties,
Morals and manners, the marine department,
Freedom of speech, and threepence for the juries.
Peisthetairus. Why, that seems all in all.
Prometheus.   Yes, everything.
I tell ye, in having her, you've everything:
I came down hastily to say thus much;
I'm hearty, ye know; I stick to principle.
Steady to the human interest—always was.
Peisthetairus. Yes! we're obliged to you for our roast victuals.
Prometheus. And I hate these present gods, you know, most
          thoroughly.
I need not tell you that.
Peisthetairus [*with a sort of half sneer*]. No, no, you need not,
You're known of old, for an enemy to the gods.
Prometheus. Yes, yes, like Timon, I'm a perfect Timon;
Just such another. But I must be going;
Give me the umbrella; if Jupiter should see me,
He'll think that I'm attending a procession.
Peisthetairus. That's well, but don't forget the folding chair,
For a part of your disguise. Here, take it with you.
                                        [*Exeunt.*

Chorus.   Beyond the navigable seas,
          Amongst the fierce Antipodes,
          There lies a lake, obscure and holy,
          Lazy, deep, melancholy,
          Solitary, secret, hidden,
          Where baths and washing are forbidden.
               Socrates, beside the brink,
          Summons from the murky sink
          Many a disembodied ghost;
          And Pisander reached the coast
          To raise the spirit that he lost;
          With a victim, strange and new,

A gawky camel, which he slew
Like Ulysses—whereupon,
The grizzly sprite of Chaerephon
Flitted round him; and appeared
With his eyebrows and his beard,
Like a strange infernal fowl,
Half a vampire, half an owl.

NEPTUNE, THE TRIBALLIAN ENVOY, HERCULES

Neptune. There's Nephelococcugia, that's the town,
   The point we're bound to, with our embassy.
            [*Turning to the Triballian.*]
   But you! What a figure have ye made yourself!
   What a way to wear a mantle! slouching off
   From the left shoulder! Hitch it round, I tell ye,
   On the right side. For shame—come—so; that's better.
   These folds, too, bundled up. There, throw them round
   Even and easy—so. Why, you're a savage,
   A natural born savage. Oh! democracy!
   What will it bring us to? When such a ruffian
   Is voted into an embassy!
Triballian [*to Neptune, who is pulling his dress about*].
                        Come, hands off!

   Hands off!
Neptune.   Keep quiet, I tell ye, and hold your tongue,
   For a very beast: in all my life in heaven,
   I never saw such another—Hercules,
   I say, what shall we do? What should you think?
Hercules. What would I do? What do I think? I've told you
   Already . . . I think to throttle him—the fellow,
   Whoever he is, that's keeping us blockaded.
Neptune. Yes, my good friend; but we were sent, you know,
   To treat for a peace. Our embassy is for peace.

Hercules. That makes no difference; or if it does,
　It makes me long to throttle him the more.
Peisthetairus [*very busy, affecting not to see them*].
　Give me the Silphium spice. Where's the cheese-grater?
　Bring cheese here, somebody! Mend the charcoal fire.
Hercules. Mortal, we greet you and hail you! Three of us—
　Three deities.
Peisthetairus [*without looking up*]. But I'm engaged at present;
　A little busy, you see, mixing my sauce.
Hercules. Why sure! How can it be? what dish is this?
　Birds seemingly!
Peisthetairus [*without looking up*]. Some individual birds,
　Opposed to the popular democratic birds,
　Rendered themselves obnoxious.
Hercules. 　　　　　　　　So, you've plucked them,
　And put them into sauce, provisionally?
Peisthetairus [*looking up*]. Oh! bless me, Hercules, I'm quite
　　　　glad to see you.
　What brings you here?
Hercules. 　　　　　We're come upon an embassy
　From heaven, to put an end to this same war . . .
Servant [*to Peisthetairus*]. The cruet's empty, our oil is out.
Peisthetairus. 　　　　　　　　No matter,
　Fetch more, fetch plenty, I tell ye. We shall want it.
Hercules. For, in fact, it brings no benefit to us,
　The continuance of the war prolonging it;
　And you yourselves, by being on good terms
　Of harmony with the gods . . . why, for the future,
　You'd never need to know the want of rain,
　For water in your tanks; and we could serve ye
　With reasonable, seasonable weather,
　According as you wished it, wet or dry.
　And this is our commission coming here,
　As envoys, with authority to treat.

Peisthetairus. Well, the dispute, you know, from the
    beginning,
  Did not originate with us. The war
  (If we could hope in any way to bring you
  To reasonable terms) might be concluded.
  Our wishes, I declare it, are for peace.
  If the same wish prevails upon your part,
  The arrangement in itself is obvious.
  A retrocession on the part of Jupiter.
  The birds again to be reintegrated
  In their estate of sovereignty. This seems
  The fair result; and if we can conclude,
  I shall hope to see the ambassadors to supper.
Hercules. Well, this seems satisfactory; I consent.
Neptune [*to Hercules*]. What's come to ye? What do ye
    mean? Are ye gone mad?
  You glutton; would you ruin your own father,
  Depriving him of his ancient sovereignty?
Peisthetairus [*to Neptune*]. Indeed! And would not it be a
    better method
  For all your deities, and confirm your power,
  To leave the birds to manage things below?
  You sit there, muffled in your clouds above,
  While all mankind are shifting, skulking, lurking,
  And perjuring themselves here out of sight.
  Whereas, if you would form a steady strict
  Alliance with the birds, when any man
  (Using the common old familiar oath—
  " By Jupiter and the crow") foreswore himself,
  The crow would pick his eyes out, for his pains.
Neptune. Well, that seems plausible—that's fairly put.
Hercules. I think so, too.
Peisthetairus [*to the Triballian*]. Well, what say you?
Triballian.   Say true.

Peisthetairus. Yes. He consents, you see! But I'll explain
    now
  The services and good offices we could do you.
  Suppose a mortal made a vow, for instance,
  To any of you; then he delays and shuffles,
  And says "the gods are easy creditors."
  In such a case, we could assist ye, I say,
  To levy a fine.
Neptune [*open to conviction, but anxious to proceed on sure
    ground*].
            How would you do it? Tell me.
Peisthetairus. Why, for example, when he's counting money,
  Or sitting in the bath, we give the warrant
  To a pursuivant of ours, a kite or magpie;
  And they pounce down immediately, and distrain
  Cash or apparel, money or money's worth,
  To twice the amount of your demand upon him.
Hercules. Well, I'm for giving up the sovereignty,
  For my part.
Neptune [*convinced, but wishing to avoid responsibility, by
    voting last*].
          The Triballian, what says he?
Hercules [*aside to the Triballian, showing his fist*].
  You, sir; do you want to be well banged or not?
  Mind how you vote! Take care how you provoke me.
Triballian. Yaw, yaw. Goot, goot.
Hercules.   He's of the same opinion.
Neptune. Then, since you're both agreed, I must agree.
Hercules [*shouting to Peisthetairus, the negotiators having
    withdrawn to consult at the extremity of the stage*].
  Well, you! we've settled this concern, you see,
  About the sovereignty; we're all agreed.
Peisthetairus. Oh faith, there's one thing more, I recollect,
  Before we part; a point that I must mention.

As for dame Juno, we'll not speak of her;
I've no pretensions, Jupiter may keep her;
But for that other queen, his manager,
The sovereign goddess, her surrender to me
Is quite an article indispensable.

Neptune. Your views, I find, are not disposed for peace:
We must turn homewards.

Peisthetairus.   As you please, so be it.
Cook, mind what you're about there with the sauce;
Let's have it rich and savoury, thicken it up!

Hercules. How now, man? Neptune! are you flying off?
Must we remain at war, here, for a woman?

Neptune. But, what are we to do?

Hercules.   Do? Why, make peace.

Neptune. I pity you really! I feel quite ashamed
And sorry to see you; ruining yourself!
If anything should happen to your father,
After surrendering the sovereignty,
What's to become of you? When you yourself
Have voted away your whole inheritance:
At his decease, you must remain a beggar.

Peisthetairus [*aside to Hercules*]. Ah there! I thought so; he's
                     coming over ye;
Step here a moment! Let me speak to ye!
     Your uncle's chousing you, my poor dear friend,
You've not a farthing's worth of expectation
From what your father leaves. Ye can't inherit
By law: ye're illegitimate, ye know.

Hercules. Heigh-day! Why, what do you mean?

Peisthetairus.   I mean the fact!
Your mother was a foreigner; Minerva
Is counted an heiress, everybody knows;
How could that be, supposing her own father
To have had a lawful heir?

Hercules.   But, if my father
　　Should choose to leave the property to me,
　　In his last will?
Peisthetairus.   The law would cancel it!
　　And Neptune, he that's using all his influence
　　To work upon ye, he'd be the very first
　　To oppose ye, and oust ye, as the testator's brother.
　　　I'll tell ye what the law says, Solon's law:
　　　"A foreign heir shall not succeed,
　　　　Where there are children of the lawful breed:
　　　　But, if no native heir there be,
　　　　The kinsman nearest in degree
　　　　Shall enter on the property."
Hercules. Does nothing come to me, then? Nothing at all,
　　Of all my father leaves?
Peisthetairus.   Nothing at all,
　　I should conceive. But you perhaps can tell me.
　　Did he, your father, ever take ye with him,
　　To get ye enrolled upon the register?
Hercules. No, truly I . . . thought it strange . . . he . . .
　　　　never did.
Peisthetairus. Well, but don't think things strange. Don't
　　　　stand there, stammering,
　　Puzzling and gaping. Trust yourself to me,
　　'Tis I must make your fortune after all!
　　　If you'll reside and settle amongst us here,
　　I'll make you chief commander among the birds,
　　Captain, and Autocrat and everything.
　　Here you shall domineer and rule the roast,
　　With splendour and opulence and pigeon's milk.
Hercules [*in a more audible voice, and in a formal decided tone*].
　　I agreed with you before: I think your argument
　　Unanswerable. I shall vote for the surrender.
Peisthetairus [*to Neptune*]. And what say you?

Neptune [*firmly and vehemently*].   Decidedly I dissent.
Peisthetairus. Then it depends upon our other friend,
  It rests with the Triballian; what say you?
Triballian. Me tell you; pretty girl, grand beautiful queen,
  Give him to birds.
Hercules.   Aye, give her up, you mean.
Neptune. Mean! He knows nothing about it. He means
          nothing
  But chattering like a magpie.
Peisthetairus.   Well, " the magpies"
  He means, the magpies or the birds in general.
  The republic of the birds—their government—
  That the surrender should be made to them.
Neptune [*in great wrath*]. Well, settle it yourselves; amongst
          yourselves;
  In your own style: I've nothing more to say.
Hercules [*to Peisthetairus*].
  Come, we're agreed in fact, to grant your terms;
  But you must come, to accompany us to the sky;
  To take back this same queen, and the other matters.
Peisthetairus [*very quietly*]. It happens lucky enough, with
          this provision
  For a marriage feast. It seems prepared on purpose.
Hercules. Indeed, and it does. Suppose in the meanwhile,
  I superintend the cookery, and turn the roast,
  While you go back together.
Neptune [*with a start of surprise and disgust*].
          Turn the roast!
  A pretty employment! Won't you go with us?
Hercules. No, thank ye; I'm mighty comfortable here.
Peisthetairus. Come, give me a marriage robe; I must be
          going.

                    J. H. FRERE.

XENOPHON

In the following three extracts we have what is probably a faithful record of Socrates' opinions and way of life; but it must be remembered that Socrates' opinions do not represent the opinions of the average Athenian: they represent exactly the opposite. Socrates had much the same effect on his own countrymen as Mr. Bradlaugh had on the typical Victorian and Mr. Lenin has on the typical Georgian of our own time: in plain words, he was considered to be a mixture of fool and knave, the latter element predominating. That he was finally put to death because of his opinions is a serious blot on the otherwise good record of Athens in the way of religious and social toleration. But as a slight offset to that error may be put the many years in which he was allowed to disseminate doctrines which his contemporaries regarded as false and paradoxical and which we regard as obvious and true.

A Dinner Party

Symposium I, 2.

Of dinner parties at which Socrates was present we have full accounts both by Plato and Xenophon. The opening chapters of the latter, slightly the more realistic of the two, are here given.

IT seems to me that it is not only the serious deeds of good men which deserve record, but also their lighter moods. As a reason for this judgment I will here set down some incidents at which I myself happened to be present.

The occasion was the horse-race at the great Panathenaic festival, to which Callias, son of Hipponicus, the lover of Autolycus, had brought the lad after his victory in the pankration. As soon as the race was over, Callias started off with Autolycus and his father to his house in the Piraeus, Niceratus being also of the party. But seeing Socrates in company with Critobulus and Hermogenes and Antisthenes and Charmides, he told a servant to escort Autolycus and his friends, while he himself went up to Socrates' group, and said: "Well, I have met you at the right time! I am just going to entertain Autolycus and his father to dinner, and the splendour of the feast, methinks, will be much enhanced if my dining-room be graced by men of pure minds like yourselves rather than by generals and cavalry officers and petitioners."

To that Socrates replied: "You are always making mock of us, Callias, and regarding us with scorn. You have given large sums for wisdom's sake to Protagoras and Gorgias and Prodicus and many others, while you see that we dig and delve for ourselves in the field of knowledge."

"Hitherto, certainly," retorted Callias, "although I had much to say, I have kept my wisdom secret from you. But if you will be my guests to-day, I will give you a display of it and prove myself worthy of consideration."

Socrates and his friends thanked Callias for the invitation, as was proper, but at first were not disposed to pledge their attendance. When they saw, however, that he would be very annoyed if they did not accept, they agreed to come, and went off all together. Before dinner some took gymnastic exercise, others anointed themselves, and others had a bath: at the banquet itself, Autolycus sat on a chair by his father's side; the rest reclined as usual on couches.

Anyone reflecting on the scene would at once have been inspired by the thought that by nature there is something regal in beauty; especially if its possessor, like Autolycus, combines with it modesty and virtue. For as when a light shines out in the darkness it attracts the eyes of all, so did the beauty of Autolycus then draw towards him the gaze of the whole company; and there was no one who saw him that was not moved at heart by the sight. Some showed their emotion by a gesture, others fell into an unusual silence. All men when they are possessed by a god, whoever that god may be, seem worthy of close attention. But while other emotions incline a man to fierce looks, terrific words, and violent actions, those who are inspired by virtuous love have a kindlier expression in their eyes than most; their voices are softer, their gestures more easy and frank. And that was the effect which love then had on Callias, so that all Love's adepts looked upon him and marvelled.

The guests then took their meal in silence, as if the command had been given them by some stronger power. But presently there was a knocking at the door, and Philip the Jester bade the porter to announce him and explain the reason of his visit. " I have come," he said, " provided with everything necessary to dine at someone else's table: my servant's shoulders, too, are very sore, for he has had nothing to carry—not even a breakfast." To that Callias replied: " 'Twere a shame, friends, to grudge the man house-room. Bring him in." And with the words he looked across at Autolycus, wondering obviously what *he* thought of the joke.

So the jester came in, and standing at the door of the dining-hall, where the table was spread, addressed the company: " You are all aware that I am a professional jester. I have come here, then, on purpose; for I think it is a finer jest to arrive unforbidden at a party than to have accepted a formal invitation."

" Take your place at table, then," replied Callias. " The company have had their fill of serious thoughts, as you perceive; it is merriment, perhaps, that they somewhat lack."

The dinner proceeded, and Philip, anxious to carry out his part of the entertainment, started a funny story. To his obvious perturbation it fell completely flat, and so did the second one which, after a short interval, he tried. Whereupon he gave up his dinner, and, covering his head, fell flat on his face.

" What is the matter, Philip?" cried Callias. "Are you in pain?"

" Yes, indeed I am," he replied; " in very great pain.

Laughter is dead and I am done for. In the old days I used
to be invited to dinner, just to amuse the company and make
them laugh. But why should anyone invite me now? I could
no more hope to be serious than to go to heaven. Moreover,
no one will invite me because he expects to be invited back.
Everyone knows that dinner in my house is an unheard-of
phenomenon."

As he spoke, he began to blow his nose, and the tone of
his voice showed plainly that he was on the verge of tears.
So everyone tried to comfort him with promises of future
merriment, and bade him get on with his dinner, while
Critobulus burst into a peal of laughter at his lamentable
words. At the sound, Philip uncovered his head, and with a
"Cheer up, my soul: we have still a shot in the locker,"
fell to again.

After the tables had been removed, the drink-offering
poured, and the hymn of thanksgiving sung, the party was
enlivened by the appearance of a Syracusan with his three
assistants: the first, a clever flute-player; the next, a dancing-
girl trained to do the most marvellous tricks; the third,
a very handsome youth, who could both play the harp and
dance in a very graceful fashion: their master exhibiting
them for hire as at a show.

The girl played upon the flute and the boy upon the
harp, and both seemed to delight the company greatly, so
that Socrates remarked: "Really, Callias, you are a perfect
host. Not merely have you served us to a dinner beyond
reproach, but you provide us also with a most delightful
spectacle and music."

To that the other: "Suppose we have some perfume
brought in, that we may feast also upon its fragrance."

"No, no," said Socrates. "As one sort of robe is beautiful
on a woman, another on a man, so one sort of scent befits a
man, another a woman. No man ever anoints himself with

perfumed oil to please his fellows. And women, too (especially young brides, like the consorts of our friends here, Niceratus and Critobulus), what need have they of fragrance, being themselves compounded of it? The scent of the wrestler's oil is better for women than any perfume; sweet if present, regretted if absent. Slave and freeman, if once they anointed themselves with myrrh, straightway smell the same. But the scents that come from a freeman's striving need time and honest living, if they are to be sweet with freedom's true fragrance."

Thereupon Lycon: "That may be well enough for young people. But what scent is left for us whose athletic days are over?"

"The fragrance of true nobility," said Socrates. "And where can one obtain that unguent?"

"Not from a perfumer's shop certainly."

"Where, then?"

"Theognis has told us, when he says:

Honest friends teach honest ways; but if your comrade be a knave,
Very soon, my son, you'll lose what little wisdom you may have."

"Do you hear that, my son?" said Lycon.

"Yes, that he does," answered Socrates, "and puts it into practice too. When he set his heart on winning the pankration, he took counsel with you; and when he seeks a higher prize, he will take counsel with that teacher who seems most competent to help him in his endeavour."

At that several of the company exclaimed. "Where will he find a teacher of that?" said one. "It is not a thing that can be taught," cried another. "It can be learnt as well as anything else," retorted a third.

Then Socrates: "It seems a debatable question. Let us put it aside for another occasion. The dancing-girl, I notice, is standing ready, and they are handing her the hoops."

Thereupon the flute-player struck up a tune for her companion, and someone standing beside the dancer kept handing her hoops until she had twelve. As she took them, she danced and flung them whirling into the air, judging carefully how high she must throw them so as to catch them in turn.

At that, Socrates: "This girl's performance, friends, is one proof among many that woman's nature appears to be in no wise inferior to man's, and that she has no lack either of judgment or physical strength. Those of you, then, that have wives, need have no fear to teach them whatever you think it would be useful for them to know."

To this Antisthenes retorted: "If that is your opinion, Socrates, why do you not try and teach Xanthippe instead of living with the most shrewish of all women, present, past or future?"

"Well," said Socrates, " I have noticed that people who wish to become expert horsemen do not buy a docile but rather a spirited nag. They think, no doubt, that if they can manage a fiery steed, they will have no difficulty in dealing with the others. And so, being anxious to have intercourse with all mankind, I took her, knowing well that if I can tolerate her, I shall easily associate with anyone."

His reason was thought to be not far wide of the mark, and soon afterwards a hoop was brought in, closely set about with upright swords. Into this ring of swords and out of it again the girl threw somersaults, till the spectators began to be afraid of some mishap: but with the greatest boldness, and without any accident, she completed her performance.

Then Socrates, addressing Antisthenes by name, said: "No one in this audience, methinks, will deny now that courage is a thing which can be taught, seeing that this girl, woman though she be, leaps so boldly into a ring of swords."

I

"Yes," said Antisthenes: "it would be an excellent idea for our Syracusan friend to exhibit his girl to the authorities, and tell them that for an adequate fee he will give all Athens courage to face the foeman's spear."

At that Philip cried: "I for my part should be delighted to see our tribune Peisander learning to throw a somersault into a ring of swords. At present a slight incapacity to look the foeman's spear in the face keeps him out of the army altogether."

Just then the boy danced a measure before the company; and Socrates said: "Do you notice how yonder fair lad appears even more beautiful when aided by the gestures of the dance than he does when his body is at rest?"

"Methinks you mean to praise his dancing-master," said Charmides.

"To be sure I do," returned Socrates. "There is another thing I observed also. In the course of his dance no part of his body was left idle. His neck and his legs and his arms all got exercise. That is how a man should dance who wants to keep himself in good fettle. I should be very glad, my Syracusan friend, to learn the proper gestures from you."

"What use will you make of them?" said the Syracusan.

"I shall use them in dancing, of course," Socrates replied.

Thereupon everyone burst out laughing, and Socrates, with a very serious face, said: "You are laughing at me, are you? Is it because I wish to improve my health by exercise, and to get more enjoyment from food and sleep? Or is it because of the sort of exercise I desire? I do not want to be like a long-distance runner with thick legs and narrow shoulders, nor like a boxer with broad shoulders and thin legs. I wish to train every part of my body, and secure an equal balance of strength. Or are you laughing because, if I take to dancing, I shall have no need to look about for a wrestling-partner, or to strip my old limbs in public, but shall

find any fair-sized room sufficient for my purpose, just as
the boy here has found this dining-hall, so that in winter I
shall take my exercise under cover, and when the weather
is too hot, in the shade? Does it seem absurd to you that I wish
to reduce the somewhat excessive size of my stomach? Are
you not aware that our friend Charmides here actually
caught me dancing the other morning?"

"Yes, that I did," said Charmides. "At first I was quite
dismayed and feared you were mad. But after you had
told me what you have now again told us, I went home,
and though I could not dance myself, never having learnt
the art, I did try a similar exercise, with which I am
acquainted, and did a little sparring."

"Ah!" said Philip, "that is obviously the reason why
your shoulders and your legs seem to be just of the same
weight. If you were to put them on the scales, tops and
bottoms, as they do loaves of bread, the clerks of the market
would have no reason to fine you."

Then Callias: "Pray invite me, Socrates, when your
dancing-lessons begin. I should like to be on the other side
of the room and take them with you."

"Come," cried Philip, "pipe me a tune and I also will
give you a dance." With that he jumped up, and mimicked
the boy's and the girl's dances over again; and since the
guests had praised the boy's beauty as being enhanced by the
gestures of the dance, so he now gave a burlesque repre-
sentation, where every movement of the body was a ridiculous exaggeration of nature. For example, since the girl
had bent backwards in the shape of a wheel, he too must
bend forwards with his head down and try to do the same.
And as the boy had been applauded for exercising all his
body in the dance, so the jester now bade the flute-girl pipe
a quicker tune and started flinging all his limbs about, legs
and arms and head. When he was weary he went back to

the table and said: "Here is a proof that my dances, too, are good exercise, friends; they have given me a fine thirst; let me have a magnum, please."

"Certainly," said Callias, "we will have one too. We are thirsty with laughing at you."

At that Socrates again broke in: "My vote, too, is given for a drink. Truly does wine moisten the soul, lulling pain to sleep, even as mandragora drugs our senses, and waking merriment, as oil kindles fire. Men's bodies, methinks, are in the same case as growing plants. When God drenches these latter too abundantly, they cannot lift their heads nor catch the breeze. But if they drink in only such moisture as they like, they grow up straight and bring forth abundance of rich fruit. And it is the same with us. If we fill the cup too abundantly, our limbs and our wits will both begin soon to reel, and we shall scarce be able to breathe, much less to talk sense. But if we are bedewed with a gentle shower— to use a Gorgian metaphor—from small glasses, we shall not be constrained to drunkenness by our wine and shall be gently led to the goal of merriment."

This was carried unanimously, with a rider from Philip: "The cup-bearers are to take pattern by good charioteers, and go quicker and quicker with the cups each time round."

The Art of Love

Memorabilia iii. 11.

Theodotë, whose dialogue with Socrates is here reported by Xenophon, was an hetaira of some repute in her day, a favourite model for artists and an intimate friend of Alcibiades, whose body she buried. It will be seen that in the give-and-take of conversation she is quite able to hold her own with the great master of dialectic, and the anecdote throws some interesting side-lights on her curious profession.

There lived once in Athens a fair lady named Theodotë, whose habit it was to give her company to anyone who

could persuade her to join him. One of the company made
mention of her to Socrates, saying that the lady's beauty
quite surpassed description. "Painters," cried he, "go to
her house to paint her portrait and, as far as is decorous, she
reveals to them all her perfection."

"Well," replied Socrates, "plainly we also must go and see
her. It is impossible from mere hearsay to realise something
that beggars description."

"Quick then," said his informant, "and follow me."

So off they went at once to Theodotë, and finding her at
home, posing to a painter, they remained some time as
spectators. When the painter had finished, "Friends," said
Socrates, "ought we to be more grateful to Theodotë for
displaying to us her beauty, or she to us for having come to
see her? I suppose if this display is going to be more advan-
tageous to her, she ought to be grateful to us. But if it is we
who are going to profit by the sight, then we ought to be
grateful to her."

"A very equitable statement of the case," said one of
the company.

"Well, then," Socrates resumed, "the lady is profiting
this moment by the praise she receives from us, and when
we report what we have seen to others she will gain a further
advantage. As for ourselves, we are beginning to have a
desire to touch that which we have just now beheld; when
we are going away we shall feel the smart; and when we are
quite gone we shall be consumed with longing. So we may
reasonably say that it is we who are her servitors, and that
she accepts our service."

"Oh dear!" said Theodotë. "If that is so, it would be only
polite for me to thank you for coming to see me."

Some time afterwards Socrates noticed that the lady
herself was expensively attired, and that her mother's dress
(for her mother was in the room) and general appearance

were by no means of a humble character. There were a number of comely maidens also in attendance, showing little signs of neglect in their accoutrement, and in all respects the household was luxuriously arranged.

"Tell me, Theodotë," said he, "have you any land of your own?"

"I have not," she replied.

"You have a house, then, I suppose, which brings you in a good income?"

"No, I do not own a house."

"Have you a factory, then?"

"No, not a factory either."

"How, then, do you get what you need?"

"My friends are my fortune, when they care to be kind to me."

"By our lady, that is a fine thing to have. A flock of friends is far better than a flock of sheep, or goats, or oxen. But do you leave it to chance whether friends are to wing their way to you like flies, or do you employ some mechanical device?"

"Why, how could I find any device in this matter?"

"Surely, it would be much more natural for you to use one than it is for spiders. You know how they hunt for their living. They weave gossamer webs, I believe, and anything that comes in their way they take for food."

"Do you advise me then to weave a hunting-net?"

"No, no. You must not imagine that it is such a simple matter to catch that noble animal, a lover. Have you not noticed that even to catch such a humble thing as a hare, people use many devices? Knowing that hares are night-feeders, they provide themselves with night-dogs, and use them to hunt them down. Furthermore, as the creatures run off at daybreak, they get other dogs to scent them out and find which way they go from their feeding-ground to their forms. Again, they are swift-footed, so that they can get away in the open, and a third class of dogs must be provided to catch them in their tracks. Lastly, inasmuch as some escape even from the dogs, men set nets in their runs, so that they may fall into the meshes and be caught."

"What sort of contrivance should I use, then, in hunting for lovers?"

"You should get a man, of course, to take the place of the dog; someone able to track out and discover wealthy amateurs for you; able also to find ways of driving them into your nets."

"Nets, forsooth! What sort of nets, pray, have I?"

"One you certainly have, close enfolding and well constructed—your body. And within your body there is your heart, which teaches you the looks that charm and the words that please. It tells you to welcome true friends with a smile, and to lock out overbearing gallants; when your beloved is sick, to tend him with anxious care; when he is prospering, to share his joy: in fine, to surrender all your soul to a devout lover. I am sure you know full well how to love. Love needs a tender heart as well as soft arms. I am sure, too, that you convince your lovers of your affection for them, not by mere phrases, but by acts of love."

"Nay, nay; I do not use any such tricks."

"Well, it makes a great difference whether you approach a man in the natural and proper way. You can neither catch nor keep a lover by force. He is a creature who can only be captured and kept constant by kindness and pleasure."

"That is true."

"To begin with, then, you should only ask of your well-wishers such services as will cost them little to render, and you should requite them with favours of the same kind. Thus you will secure their fervent and constant love, and they will become your benefactors indeed. You will charm them best if you never surrender except when they are sharp-set. You have noticed that the daintiest fare, if served before a man wants it, is apt to seem insipid; while, if he is already sated, it even produces a feeling of nausea. Create a hunger before you bring on your banquet: then even humble food will seem delicious."

"How can I create this hunger in my friends?"

"Firstly, never serve them when they are sated. Never suggest it even. Wait until the sense of repletion has quite passed away, and they begin again to be sharp-set. Even then, at first, let your suggestions be only of most modest conversation. Seem not to wish to yield. Fly from them—and fly again: until they feel the keen pang of hunger. That is your moment. The gift is the same as when the man did not want it: but wondrous different now its value."

"Why do you not join me, Socrates, in the hunt and help me to catch lovers?"

"I will, if you can persuade me."

"But how can I?"

"You must look yourself and find a way, if you want me."

"Come to my house, then, often."

Thereat Socrates, jesting at his own indifference to business, replied: "It is no easy matter for me to take a holiday. I have a hundred affairs, private and public, to occupy me. Moreover, there are my lady friends, who will never let me leave them, night or day. They would always be having me teach them love-charms and incantations."

"Are you really acquainted with such things, Socrates?"

"Of course I am. What else is the reason, think you, that Apollodorus and Antisthenes never leave my side? Why have Cebes and Simmias come all the way from Thebes to stay with me? You may be quite sure that not without love-charms and incantations and magic-wheels can this be brought about."

"Lend me your wheel, then, that I may use it on you."

"Nay, I do not want to be drawn to you. I want you to come to me."

"Well, I will come. But be sure and be at home."

" I will be at home to you, unless there be some lady with me who is dearer even than yourself."

The Art of Marriage

Oeconomicus 7–10.

As a pendant to his sketch of free-love and a rather exceptional woman, Xenophon gives us here a more elaborate picture of marriage and a very exceptional man.

It chanced, one day I saw him seated in the portico of Zeus Eleutherios, and as he appeared to be at leisure, I went up to him and, sitting down by his side, accosted him: How is this, Ischomachus? you seated here, you who are so little wont to be at leisure? As a rule, when I see you, you are doing something, or at any rate not sitting idle in the market-place.

Nor would you see me now so sitting, Socrates (he answered), but that I promised to meet some strangers, friends of mine, at this place.

And when you have no such business on hand (I said), where in heaven's name do you spend your time and how do you employ yourself? I will not conceal from you how anxious I am to learn from your own lips by what conduct you have earned for yourself the title " beautiful and good." It is not by spending your days indoors at home, I am sure; the whole habit of your body bears witness to a different sort of life.

Then Ischomachus, smiling at my question, but also, as it seemed to me, a little pleased to be asked what he had done to earn the title " beautiful and good," made answer: Whether that is the title by which folk call me when they talk to you about me, I cannot say; all I know is, when they challenge me to exchange properties, or else to perform some service to the state instead of them, the fitting out of a trireme or the training of a chorus, nobody thinks of asking for the beautiful and good gentleman, but it is plain Ischomachus, the son of So-and-so, upon whom the summons is served. But to answer your question, Socrates (he proceeded), I certainly do not spend my days indoors, if for no other reason, because my wife is quite capable of managing our domestic affairs without my aid.

Ah! (said I), Ischomachus, that is just what I should like particularly to learn from you. Did you yourself educate your wife to be all that a wife should be, or when you received her from her father and mother was she already a proficient well skilled to discharge the duties appropriate to a wife?

Well skilled! (he replied). What proficiency was she likely to bring with her, when she was not quite fifteen at the time she wedded me, and during the whole prior period of her life had been most carefully brought up to see and hear as little as possible, and to ask the fewest questions? or do you not think one should be satisfied, if at marriage her whole experience consisted in knowing how to take the wool and make a dress, and seeing how her mother's handmaidens had their daily spinning-tasks assigned them? For (he added), as regards control of appetite and self-indulgence, she had received the soundest education, and that I take to be the most important matter in the bringing-up of man or woman.

Then all else (said I) you taught your wife yourself, Ischomachus, until you had made her capable of attending carefully to her appointed duties?

That did I not (replied he) until I had offered sacrifice, and prayed that I might teach and she might learn all that could conduce to the happiness of us twain.

Socrates. And did your wife join in sacrifice and prayer to that effect?

Ischomachus. Most certainly, with many a vow registered to heaven to become all she ought. to be; and her whole manner showed that she would not be neglectful of what was taught her.

Socrates. Pray narrate to me, Ischomachus, I beg of you, what you first essayed to teach her. To hear that story would please me more than any description of the most splendid gymnastic contest or horse-race you could give me.

Why, Socrates (he answered), when after a time she had become accustomed to my hand, that is, was tamed sufficiently to play her part in a discussion, I put to her this question: " Did it ever strike you to consider, dear wife, what led me to choose you as my wife among all women, and your parents to entrust you to me of all men? It was certainly not from any difficulty that might beset either of us to find another bedfellow. That I am sure is evident to you. No! it was with deliberate intent to discover, I for myself and your parents in behalf of you, the best partner of house and children we could find, that I sought you out, and your parents, acting to the best of their ability, made choice of me. If at some future time God grant us to have children born to us, we will take counsel together how best to bring them up, for that too will be a common interest, and a common blessing if haply they shall live to fight our battles and we find in them hereafter support and succour when ourselves are old. But at present there is our house here, which belongs alike to both. It is common property, for all that I possess goes by my will into the common fund, and in the same way all that you deposited was placed by you to the common fund. We need not stop to calculate in figures which of us contributed most, but rather let us lay to heart this fact, that whichever of us proves the better partner, he or she at once contributes what is most worth having."

Thus I addressed her, Socrates, and thus my wife made

answer: "But how can I assist you? what is my ability? Nay, everything depends on you. My business, my mother told me, was to be sober-minded!"

"Most true, my wife," I replied, "and that is what my father said to me. But what is the proof of sober-mindedness in man or woman? Is it not so to behave that what they have of good may ever be at its best, and that new treasures from the same source of beauty and righteousness may be most amply added?"

"But what is there that I can do," my wife inquired, "which will help to increase our joint estate?"

"Assuredly," I answered, "you may strive to do as well as possible what Heaven has given you a natural gift for, and which the law approves."

"And what may these things be?" she asked.

"To my mind they are not the things of least importance," I replied, "unless the things which the queen-bee in her hive presides over are of slight importance to the bee community; for the gods" (so Ischomachus assured me, he continued), "the gods, my wife, would seem to have exercised much care and judgment in compacting that twin-system which goes by the name of male and female, so as to secure the greatest possible advantage to the pair. Since no doubt the underlying principle of the bond is first and foremost to perpetuate through procreation the races of living creatures; and next, as the outcome of this bond, for human beings at any rate, a provision is made by which they may have sons and daughters to support them in old age.

"And again, the way of life of human beings, not being maintained like that of cattle in the open-air, obviously demands roofed homesteads. But if these same human beings are to have anything to bring in under cover, some one to carry out these labours of the field under high heaven must be found them, since such operations as the breaking up of fallow with the plough, the sowing of seed, the planting of trees, the pasturing and herding of flocks, are one and all open-air employments on which the supply of products necessary to life depends.

"As soon as these products of the field are safely housed and under cover, new needs arise. There must be some one to guard the store and some one to perform such operations as imply the need of shelter. Shelter, for instance, is needed for the rearing of infant children; shelter is needed for the various processes of converting the fruits of earth into food, and in like manner for the fabrication of clothing out of wool.

" But whereas both of these, the indoor and the outdoor occupations alike, demand new toil and new attention, to meet the case," I added, "God made provision from the first by shaping, as it seems to me, the woman's nature for indoor and the man's for outdoor occupations. Man's body and soul He furnished with a greater capacity for enduring heat and cold, wayfaring and military marches; or, to repeat, He laid upon his shoulders the outdoor works.

" While in creating the body of woman with less capacity for these things," I continued, "God would seem to have imposed on her the indoor works; and knowing that He had implanted in the woman and imposed upon her the nurture of new-born babes, He endowed her with a larger share of affection for the new-born child than He bestowed upon man. And since He had imposed on woman the guardianship of the things imported from without, God, in His wisdom, perceiving that a fearful spirit was no detriment to guardianship, endowed the woman with a larger measure of timidity than He bestowed on man. Knowing further that he to whom the outdoor works belonged would need to defend them against malign attack, He endowed the man in turn with a larger share of courage.

"And seeing that both alike feel the need of giving and receiving, He set down memory and carefulness between them for their common use, so that you would find it hard to determine whether of the two, the male or the female, has the larger share of these. So, too, God set down between them for their common use the gift of self-control, where needed, adding only to that one of the twain, whether man or woman, which should prove the better, the power to be rewarded with a larger share of this perfection. And for the very reason that their natures are not alike adapted to like ends, they stand in greater need of one another; and the married couple is made more useful to itself, the one fulfilling what the other lacks.

"Now, being well aware of this, my wife," I added, "and knowing well what things are laid upon us twain by God Himself, must we not strive to perform, each in the best way possible, our respective duties? Law, too, gives her consent—law and the usage of mankind, by sanctioning the wedlock of man and wife; and just as God ordained them to be partners in their children, so the law establishes their common ownership of house and estate. Custom, moreover, proclaims as beautiful those excellences of man and woman with which God gifted them at birth. Thus for a woman to bide tranquilly at home rather than roam abroad is no dishonour; but for a man to remain indoors, instead of devoting himself to outdoor pursuits, is a thing discreditable. But if a man does things contrary to the nature given him by God, the chances are, such insubordination escapes not the eye of Heaven: he pays the penalty, whether of neglecting his own works, or of performing those appropriate to woman."

I added: "Just such works, if I mistake not, that same queen-bee we spoke of labours hard to perform, like yours, my wife, enjoined upon her by God Himself."

"And what sort of works are these?" she asked; "what

has the queen-bee to do that she seems so like myself, or I like her in what I have to do?"

"Why," I answered, "she too stays in the hive and suffers not the other bees to idle. Those whose duty it is to work outside she sends forth to their labours; and all that each of them brings in, she notes and receives and stores against the day of need; but when the season for use has come, she distributes a just share to each. Again, it is she who presides over the fabric of choicely-woven cells within. She looks to it that warp and woof are wrought with speed and beauty. Under her guardian eye the brood of young is nursed and reared; but when the days of rearing are past and the young bees are ripe for work, she sends them out as colonists with one of the seed royal to be their leader."

"Shall I then have to do these things?" asked my wife.

"Yes," I answered, "you will need in the same way to stay indoors, despatching to their toils without those of your domestics whose work lies there. Over those whose appointed tasks are wrought indoors, it will be your duty to preside; yours to receive the stuffs brought in; yours to apportion part for daily use, and yours to make provision for the rest, to guard and garner it so that the outgoings destined for a year may not be expended in a month. It will be your duty, when the wools are introduced, to see that clothing is made for those who need; your duty also to see that the dried corn is rendered fit and serviceable for food.

"There is just one of all these occupations which devolve upon you," I added, "you may not find so altogether pleasing. Should any of our household fall sick, it will be your care to see and tend them to the recovery of their health."

"Nay," she answered, "that will be my pleasantest of tasks, if careful nursing may touch the springs of gratitude and leave them friendlier than heretofore."

And I (continued Ischomachus) was struck with admiration at her answer, and replied: "Think you, my wife, it is through some such traits of forethought seen in their mistress-leader that the hearts of bees are won, and they are so loyally affectioned towards her that, if ever she abandon her hive, not one of them will dream of being left behind; but one and all must follow her."

And my wife made answer to me: "It would much astonish me (said she) did not these leader's works, you speak of, point to you rather than to myself. Methinks mine would be a pretty guardianship and distribution of things indoors without your provident care to see that the importations from without were duly made."

"Just so," I answered, "and mine would be a pretty importation if there were no one to guard what I imported. Do you not see," I added, "how pitiful is the case of those unfortunates who pour water into their sieves for ever, as the story goes, and labour but in vain?"

"Pitiful enough, poor souls," she answered, "if that is what they do."

"But there are other cares, you know, and occupations," I answered, "which are yours by right, and these you will find agreeable. This, for instance: to take some maiden who knows naught of carding wool and to make her a proficient in the art, doubling her usefulness; or to receive another quite ignorant of housekeeping or of service, and to render her skilful, loyal, serviceable, till she is worth her weight in gold; or again, when occasion serves, you have it in your power to requite by kindness the well-behaved whose presence is a blessing to your house; or maybe to chasten the bad character, should such an one appear. But the greatest joy of all will be to prove yourself my better; to make me your faithful follower; knowing no dread lest as the years advance you should decline in honour in your household, but rather trusting that, though your hair turn grey, yet, in proportion as you come to be a better helpmate to myself and to the children, a better guardian of our home, so will your honour increase throughout the household as mistress, wife, and mother, daily more dearly prized. Since," I added, "it is not through excellence of outward form, but by reason of the lustre of virtues shed forth upon the life of man, that increase is given to things beautiful and good."

That, Socrates, or something like that, as far as I may trust my memory, records the earliest conversation which I held with her.

And did you happen to observe, Ischomachus (I asked), whether, as the result of what was said, your wife was stirred at all to greater carefulness?

Yes, certainly (Ischomachus answered); and I remember how piqued she was one time and how deeply she blushed, when I chanced to ask her for something which had been brought into the house, and she could not give it me. So I, when I saw her annoyance, fell to consoling her. " Do not be at all disheartened, my wife, that you cannot give me what I ask for. It is plain poverty, no doubt, to need a thing and not to have the use of it. But as wants go, to look for something which I cannot lay my hands upon is a less painful form of indigence than never to dream of looking, because I know full well the thing exists not. Anyhow, you are not to blame for this," I added; " mine the fault was who handed over to your care the things without assigning them their places. Had I done so, you would have known not only where to put but where to find them. After all, my wife, there is nothing in human life so serviceable, nought so beautiful as order.

" For instance, what is a chorus?—a band composed of human beings, who dance and sing; but suppose the company proceed to act as each may chance,—confusion

K

follows; the spectacle has lost its charm. How different when each and all together act and recite with orderly precision, the limbs and voices keeping time and tune. Then, indeed, these same performers are worth seeing and worth hearing.

"So, too, an army," I said, "my wife, an army destitute of order is confusion worse confounded: to enemies an easy prey, courting attack; to friends a bitter spectacle of wasted power; a mingled mob of asses, heavy infantry, and baggage-bearers, light infantry, cavalry, and waggons. Now, suppose they are on the march; how are they to get along? In this condition everybody will be a hindrance to everybody: 'slow march' side by side with 'double quick,' 'quick march' at cross purposes with 'stand at ease'; waggons blocking cavalry and asses fouling waggons; baggage-bearers and hoplites jostling together: the whole a hopeless jumble. And when it comes to fighting, such an army is not precisely in condition to deliver battle. The troops who are compelled to retreat before the enemy's advance are fully capable of trampling down the heavy infantry detachments in reserve.

"How different is an army well organised in battle order: a splendid sight for friendly eyes to gaze at, albeit an eyesore to the enemy. For who, being of their party, but will feel a thrill of satisfaction as he watches the serried masses of heavy infantry moving onwards in unbroken order? who but will gaze with wonderment as the squadrons of the cavalry dash past him at the gallop? And what of the foeman? will not his heart sink within him to see the orderly arrangements of the different arms: here heavy infantry and cavalry, and there again light infantry, there archers and there slingers, following each their leaders with orderly precision. As they tramp onwards thus in order, though they number many myriads, yet even so they move on and on in quiet

progress, stepping like one man, and the place just vacated
in front is filled up on the instant from the rear.

"Or picture a trireme, crammed choke-full of mariners;
for what reason is she so terror-striking an object to her
enemies, and a sight so gladsome to the eyes of friends? is
it not that the gallant ship sails so swiftly? And why is it
that, for all their crowding, the ship's company cause each
other no distress? Simply that there, as you may see them,
they sit in order; in order bend to the oar; in order recover
the stroke; in order step on board; in order disembark. But
disorder is, it seems to me, precisely as though a man who is
a husbandman should stow away together in one place wheat
and barley and pulse, and by and by when he has need of
barley meal, or wheaten flour, or some condiment of pulse,
then he must pick and choose instead of laying his hand on
each thing separately sorted for use.

"And so with you too, my wife, if you would avoid this
confusion, if you would fain know how to administer our
goods, so as to lay your finger readily on this or that as you
may need, or if I ask you for anything, graciously to give it
me: let us, I say, select and assign the appropriate place for
each set of things. This shall be the place where we will put
the things; and we will instruct the housekeeper that she is
to take them out thence, and mind to put them back again
there; and in this way we shall know whether they are safe
or not. If anything is gone, the gaping space will cry out as
if it asked for something back. The mere look and aspect
of things will argue what wants mending; and the fact of
knowing where each thing is will be like having it put into
one's hand at once to use without further trouble or debate."

I must tell you, Socrates, what strikes me as the finest
and most accurate arrangement of goods and furniture it
was ever my fortune to set eyes on; when I went as a sight-
seer on board the great Phoenician merchantman, and

beheld an endless quantity of goods and gear of all sorts, all separately packed and stowed away within the smallest compass. I need scarce remind you (he said, continuing his narrative) what a vast amount of wooden spars and cables a ship depends on in order to get to moorings; or again, in putting out to sea; you know the host of sails and cordage, rigging as they call it, she requires for sailing; the quantity of engines and machinery of all sorts she is armed with in case she should encounter any hostile craft; the infinitude of arms she carries, with her crew of fighting men aboard. Then all the vessels and utensils, such as people use at home on land, required ⸢for the different messes, form a portion of the freight; and besides all this, the hold is heavy laden with a mass of merchandise, the cargo proper, which the master carries with him for the sake of traffic.

Well, all these different things that I have named lay packed there in a space but little larger than a fair-sized dining-room. The several sorts, moreover, as I noticed, lay so well arranged, there could be no entanglement of one with other, nor were searchers needed; and if all were snugly stowed, all were alike get-at-able, much to the avoidance of delay if anything were wanted on the instant.

Then the pilot's mate—"the look-out man at the prow," to give him his proper title—was, I found, so well acquainted with the place for everything that, even off the ship, he could tell you where each set of things was laid and how many there were of each, just as well as any one who knows his alphabet could tell you how many letters there are in *Socrates* and the order in which they stand.

I saw this same man (continued Ischomachus) examining at leisure everything which could possibly be needful for the service of the ship. His inspection caused me such surprise, I asked him what he was doing, whereupon he answered, "I am inspecting, stranger," "just considering," says he, "the

way the things are lying aboard the ship; in case of accidents,
you know, to see if anything is missing, or not lying snug
and shipshape. There is no time left, you know," he added,
"when God makes a tempest in the great deep, to set about
searching for what you want, or to be giving out anything
which is not snug and shipshape in its place. God threatens
and chastises sluggards. If only He destroy not innocent with
guilty, a man may be content; or if He turn and save all
hands aboard that render right good service, thanks be
to Heaven."

So spoke the pilot's mate; and I, with this carefulness of
stowage still before my eyes, proceeded to enforce my thesis:

"Stupid in all conscience would it be on our parts, my wife,
if those who sail the sea in ships, that are but small things,
can discover space and place for everything; can, moreover,
in spite of violent tossings up and down, keep order, and,
even while their hearts are failing them for fear, find everything they need to hand; whilst we, with all our ample store-
rooms diversely disposed for divers objects in our mansion,
an edifice firmly based on solid ground, fail to discover fair
and fitting places, easy of access for our several goods! Would
not that argue great lack of understanding in our two selves?
Well then! how good a thing it is to have a fixed and orderly
arrangement of all furniture and gear; how easy also in a
dwelling-house to find a place for every sort of goods, in
which to stow them as shall suit each best,—needs no further
comment. Rather let me harp upon the string of beauty—
image a fair scene: the boots and shoes and sandals, and so
forth, all laid in order, row upon row; the cloaks, the mantles,
and the rest of the apparel stowed in their own places; the
coverlets and bedding; the copper caldrons; and all the
articles for table use! Nay, though it well may raise a smile
of ridicule (not on the lips of a grave man perhaps, but of
some facetious witling) to hear me say it, a beauty like the

cadence of sweet music dwells even in pots and pans set out in neat array: and so, in general, fair things ever show more fair when orderly bestowed. The separate atoms shape themselves to form a choir, and all the space between gains beauty by their banishment. Even so some sacred chorus, dancing a roundelay in honour of Dionysus, not only is a thing of beauty in itself, but the whole interspace swept clean of dancers owns a separate charm

"The truth of what I say, we easily can test, my wife," I added, "by direct experiment, and that too without cost at all or even serious trouble. Nor need you now distress yourself, my wife, to think how hard it will be to discover some one who has wit enough to learn the places for the several things and memory to take and place them there. We know, I fancy, that the goods of various sorts contained in this whole city far outnumber ours many thousand times; and yet you have only to bid any one of your domestics go buy this, or that, and bring it you from market, and not one of them will hesitate. The whole world knows both where to go and where to find each thing.

"And why is this?" I asked. "Merely because they lie in an appointed place. But now, if you are seeking for a human being, and that too at times when he is seeking you on his side also, often and often shall you give up the search in sheer despair: and of this again the reason? Nothing else save that no appointed place was fixed where one was to await the other." Such, so far as I can now recall it, was the conversation which we held together touching the arrangement of our various chattels and their uses.

Well (I replied), and did your wife appear, Ischomachus, to lend a willing ear to what you tried thus earnestly to teach her?

Ischomachus. Most certainly she did, with promise to pay all attention. Her delight was evident, like some one's who

at length had found a pathway out of difficulties; in proof of
which she begged me to lose no time in making the orderly
arrangement I had spoken of.

And how did you introduce the order she demanded,
Ischomachus? (I asked).

Ischomachus. Well, first of all, I thought I ought to show
her the capacities of our house. Since you must know, it is
not decked with ornaments and fretted ceilings, Socrates;
but the rooms were built expressly with a view to forming
the most apt receptacles for whatever was intended to be
put in them, so that the very look of them proclaimed what
suited each particular chamber best. Thus our own bedroom,
secure in its position like a stronghold, claimed possession
of our choicest carpets, coverlets, and other furniture. Thus,
too, the warm dry rooms would seem to ask for our stock of
bread-stuffs; the chill cellar for our wine; the bright and
well-lit chambers for whatever works or furniture required
light, and so forth.

Next I proceeded to point out to her the several dwelling-
rooms, all beautifully fitted up for cool in summer and for
warmth in winter. I showed her how the house enjoyed a
southern aspect, whence it was plain, in winter it would
catch the sunlight and in summer lie in shade. Then I
showed her the women's apartments, separated from the
men's apartments by a bolted door, whereby nothing from
within could be conveyed without clandestinely, nor children
born and bred by our domestics without our knowledge and
consent—no unimportant matter, since, if the act of rearing
children tends to make good servants still more loyally
disposed, cohabiting but sharpens ingenuity for mischief
in the bad.

When we had gone over all the rooms (he continued),
we at once set about distributing our furniture in classes;
and we began (he said) by collecting everything we use in

offering sacrifice. After this we proceeded to set apart the ornaments and holiday attire of the wife, and the husband's clothing both for festivals and war; then the bedding used in the women's apartments, and the bedding used in the men's apartments; then the women's shoes and sandals, and the shoes and sandals of the men. There was one division devoted to arms and armour; another to instruments used for carding wool; another to implements for making bread; another to utensils for cooking condiments; another to utensils for the bath; another connected with the kneading trough; another with the service of the table. All these we assigned to separate places, distinguishing one portion for daily and recurrent use and the rest for high days and holidays. Next we selected and set aside the supplies required for the month's expenditure; and, under a separate head, we stored away what we computed would be needed for the year. For in this way there is less chance of failing to note how the supplies are likely to last to the end.

And so having arranged the different articles of furniture in classes, we proceeded to convey them to their appropriate places. That done, we directed our attention to the various articles needed by our domestics for daily use, such as implements or utensils for making bread, cooking relishes, spinning wool, and anything else of the same sort. These we consigned to the care of those who would have to use them, first pointing out where they must stow them, and enjoining on them to return them safe and sound when done with.

As to the other things which we should only use on feast-days, or for the entertainment of guests, or on other like occasions at long intervals, we delivered them one and all to our housekeeper. Having pointed out to her their proper places, and having numbered and registered the several sets of articles, we explained that it was her business to give out each thing as required; to recollect to whom she gave them; and when she got them back, to restore them severally to the places from which she took them. In appointing our housekeeper, we had taken every pains to discover some one on whose self-restraint we might depend, not only in the matters of food and wine and sleep, but also in her intercourse with men. She must besides, to please us, be gifted with no ordinary memory. She must have sufficient forethought not to incur displeasure through neglect of our interests. It must be her object to gratify us in this or that, and in return to win esteem and honour at our hands. We set ourselves to teach and train her to feel a kindly disposition towards us, by allowing her to share our joys in the day of gladness, or, if aught unkind befell us, by inviting her to sympathise in our sorrow. We sought to rouse in her a zeal for our interests, an eagerness to promote the increase of our estate, by making her intelligent of its affairs, and by giving her a share in our successes. We instilled in her a sense of justice and uprightness, by holding the just in higher honour than the unjust, and by pointing out that the lives of the righteous are richer and less servile than those of the unrighteous; and this was the position in which she found herself installed in our household.

And now, on the strength of all that we had done, Socrates (he added), I addressed my wife, explaining that all these things would fail of use unless she took in charge herself to see that the order of each several part was kept. Thereupon I taught her that in every well-constituted city the citizens are not content merely to pass good laws, but they further choose them *guardians of the laws*, whose function as inspectors is to praise the man whose acts are law-abiding, or to mulct some other who offends against the law. Accordingly, I bade her believe that she, the mistress, was herself to play the part of guardian of the laws to her whole household, examining whenever it seemed good to her, and passing in review the several chattels, just as the officer in command of a garrison musters and reviews his men. She must apply her scrutiny and see that everything was well, even as the Senate tests the condition of the Knights and of their horses. Like a queen, she must bestow, according to the power vested in her, praise and honour on the well-deserving, but blame and chastisement on him who stood in need thereof.

Nor did my lessons end here (added he); I taught her that she must not be annoyed should I seem to be enjoining upon her more trouble than upon any of our domestics with regard to our possessions; pointing out to her that these domestics have only so far a share in their master's chattels that they must fetch and carry, tend and guard them; nor have they the right to use a single one of them except the master grant it. But to the master himself all things pertain to use as he thinks best. And so I pointed the conclusion: he to whom the greater gain attaches in the preservation of the property or loss in its destruction, is surely he to whom by right belongs the larger measure of attention.

What, then (I asked), Ischomachus, how fared it? was your wife disposed at all to lend a willing ear to what you told her?

Bless you, Socrates (he answered), what did she do but forthwith answer me, I formed a wrong opinion if I fancied that, in teaching her the need of minding our property, I was imposing a painful task upon her. A painful task it might have been (she added), had I bade her neglect her personal concerns! But to be obliged to fulfil the duty of attending to her own domestic happiness, that was easy. After all it would seem to be but natural (added he); just as any honest woman finds it easier to care for her own offspring than to neglect them, so, too, he could well believe, an honest woman might find it pleasanter to care for than to neglect possessions, the very charm of which is that they are one's very own.

So (continued Socrates), when I heard his wife had made this answer, I exclaimed: By Hera, Ischomachus, a brave and masculine intelligence the lady has, as you describe her.

(To which Ischomachus) Yes, Socrates, and I would fain narrate some other instances of like large-mindedness on her part: shown in the readiness with which she listened to my words and carried out my wishes.

What sort of thing? (I answered). Do, pray, tell me, since I would far more gladly learn about a living woman's virtues than that Zeuxis should show me the portrait of the loveliest woman he has painted.

Whereupon Ischomachus proceeded to narrate as follows: I must tell you, Socrates, I one day noticed she was much enamelled with white lead, no doubt to enhance the natural whiteness of her skin; she had rouged herself with alkanet profusely, doubtless to give more colour to her cheeks than truth would warrant; she was wearing high-heeled shoes, in order to seem taller than she was by nature.

Accordingly I put to her this question: "Tell me, my wife, would you esteem me a less lovable co-partner in our wealth, were I to show you how our fortune stands exactly, without boasting of unreal possessions or concealing what we really have? Or would you prefer that I should try to cheat you with exaggeration, exhibiting false money to you, or sham necklaces, or flaunting purples which will lose their colour, stating they are genuine the while?"

She caught me up at once. "Hush, hush!" she said, "talk not such talk. May heaven forfend that you should ever be like that. I could not love you with my whole heart were you really of that sort."

"And are we two not come together," I continued,

"for a closer partnership, being each a sharer in the other's body?"

"That, at any rate, is what folk say," she answered.

"Then as regards this bodily relation," I proceeded, "should you regard me as more lovable or less did I present myself, my one endeavour and my sole care being that my body should be hale and strong and thereby well complexioned, or would you have me first anoint myself with pigments, smear my eyes with patches of 'true flesh colour,' and so seek your embrace, like a cheating consort presenting to his mistress's sight and touch vermilion paste instead of his own flesh?"

"Frankly," she answered, "it would not please me better to touch paste than your true self. Rather would I see your own 'true flesh colour' than any pigment of that name; would liefer look into your eyes and see them radiant with health than washed with any wash, or dyed with any ointment there may be."

"Believe the same, my wife, of me then," Ischomachus continued (so he told me); "believe that I too am not better pleased with white enamel or with alkanet than with your own natural hue; but as the gods have fashioned horses to delight in horses, cattle in cattle, sheep in their fellow sheep, so to human beings the human body pure and undefiled is sweetest; and as to these deceits, though they may serve to cheat the outside world without detection, yet if intimates try to deceive each other, they must one day be caught: in rising from their beds, before they make their toilet; by a drop of sweat they stand convicted; tears are an ordeal they cannot pass; the bath reveals them as they truly are."

What answer (said I) did she make, in Heaven's name, to what you said?

What, indeed (replied the husband), save only, that thenceforward she never once indulged in any practice of the sort,

but has striven to display the natural beauty of her person
in its purity. She did, however, put to me a question: Could
I advise her how she might become not in false show but
really fair to look upon?

This, then, was the counsel which I gave her, Socrates:
Not to be for ever seated like a slave; but, with Heaven's
help, to assume the attitude of a true mistress standing before
the loom, and where her knowledge gave her the superiority,
bravely to give the aid of her instruction; where her knowledge failed, as bravely try to learn. I counselled her to
oversee the baking woman as she made the bread; to stand
beside the housekeeper as she measured out her stores; to
go tours of inspection to see if all things were in order as
they should be. For, as it seemed to me, this would at once
be walking exercise and supervision. And, as an excellent
gymnastic, I recommended her to knead the dough and roll
the paste; to shake the coverlets and make the beds; adding,
if she trained herself in exercise of this sort she would enjoy
her food, grow vigorous in health, and her complexion
would in very truth be lovelier. The very look and aspect
of the wife, the mistress, seen in rivalry with that of her
attendants, being as she is at once more fair and more be-
comingly adorned, has an attractive charm, and not the less
because her acts are acts of grace, not services enforced.
Whereas your ordinary fine lady, seated in solemn state,
would seem to court comparison with painted counterfeits
of womanhood

And, Socrates, I would have you know that still to-day
my wife is living in a style as simple as that I taught her then,
and now recount to you.

H. G. DAKYNS.

THE ATTIC ORATORS

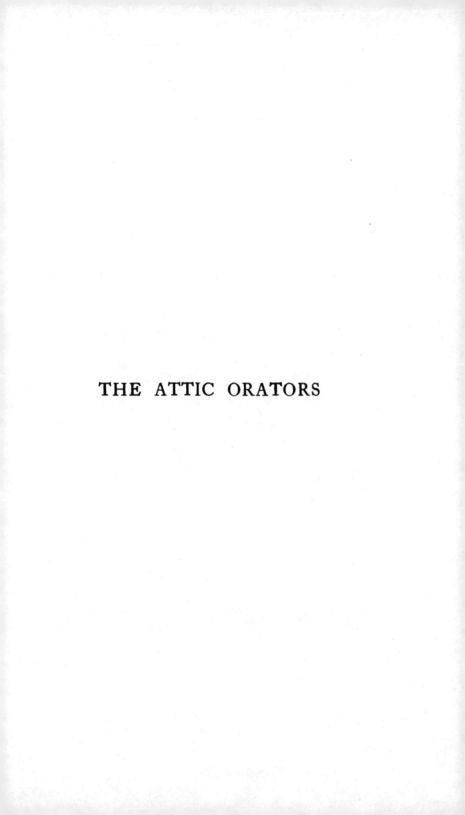

THE ATTIC ORATORS

It is in the Law Courts that the weaknesses of any social system are most clearly revealed; and it is in the law reports that the student of social science finds his most valuable material. The fact holds as much for ancient Athens as for modern England, and the speeches of the ten orators who comprise the Attic canon are our richest mine of information as regards the habits and customs of the Athenians, their modes of life and their ways of thought. It is true that any question of fact must be received with caution when it rests merely on the evidence of these ingenious pleaders: it by no means follows that a statement is true because it is made by Isaeus or Demosthenes. But with this proviso—and even their lies are useful as showing the sort of thing that was thought likely to deceive a jury—more instruction as to the actual facts of life at Athens can be extracted from the orators than from any other source, save perhaps Aristophanes.

ANTIPHON

Against the Step-mother

ANTIPHON.

The speech attributed to Antiphon, "A charge of poisoning by a step-mother," brings up in rather a striking fashion the belief commonly held both in Greek and Roman society, that love could be secured by the administration of drugs. It was realised that these substances were uncertain and dangerous in their operation, often causing madness or death, and the Latin word for poison, "venenum," is probably derived from Venus, the goddess of love. But whether the giving of a love-potion constitutes legal murder, is a point which in this speech is not considered. The case is brought by the dead man's son against his step-brothers, representing their mother, whose name is not given. The chief actors in the domestic drama unfolded to the jury are the father's wife, the father's friend

L   143

(Philoneos), and the unfortunate slave-girl, who is made the wife's unwitting instrument. The only positive evidence against the defendant is her refusal to surrender her household servants for examination under torture, and no witnesses are called.

I am a young man, gentlemen, without any legal experience, and my position is one of extreme and painful difficulty. On the one hand my father enjoined me to prosecute his murderers, and I cannot disobey him: on the other hand, by so doing I must inevitably set myself at variance with those who should be nearest and dearest to me, my step-brothers, I mean, and their mother. Fate and their own action has compelled me to bring this action against the very persons who ought properly to have shown themselves avengers of the dead man and helpers in this prosecution. They have preferred to take the opposite course; they have come forward themselves as my opponents and, as I and this indictment aver, they have rendered themselves guilty of murder.

If then, gentlemen, I can prove to you that these men's mother acted with forethought and premeditation and was our father's murderess, and that, not once only but many times before that day, she was caught in the very process of devising his death, I beg you to appear as champions of your own laws, which you have received from the gods and our ancestors, and in accordance with them to give your verdict for a conviction. I beg you also to come to the assistance of the dead man, and with him of me, who am now left quite alone. You are the only friends to whom I can appeal. Those who should have avenged the dead and helped me have made themselves his murderers and are opposing me here in court. Where, then, can a man look for assistance; with whom shall he take refuge, save with you and with Justice?

As regards my brother, I cannot understand his motives in appearing against me. Does he think it a pious duty not to abandon his mother? I, for my part, think the impiety rather lies in remitting vengeance for the dead, especially when his death was involuntary and the result of treachery, while she of her own accord plotted to kill him. He cannot say: "I am quite sure my mother did not kill our father." He could have got definite knowledge by submitting some of his slaves to torture; but he refused to do so, although he was eager enough to use that expedient on others, who had nothing to tell. He ought to have accepted my challenge and used every effort to find out how the facts really stood. If the slaves had not agreed in their confession, then he could have been quite sure in his defence, and put forward every effort against me; and on this charge his mother would have been acquitted. But seeing that he has refused to put things to a test, how is it permissible for him to say he is sure of matters into which he would not consent to inquire? What defence does he intend to offer, I wonder? If the slaves had been examined under torture, he knew well that she must be convicted, and the best chance of safety, as he thought, was to refuse to have them questioned; the true facts, as they considered, having been obscured in process of time. How then can we regard this affidavit as true, if he pretends that he is quite sure of her innocence? He refused to obtain definite information, while I was willing in this matter to adopt the most formal methods of examination by torture. I wanted to question their slaves who knew that in the past this woman, my opponents' mother, planned our father's death by means of poison, that our father caught her in the act, and that she did not deny it, save only that she alleged that the drug was a love-potion and was not meant to kill. Accordingly, I offered to set on record the charges I am making against this woman, and then let them conduct the examination. They themselves were to put the questions to the slaves in my presence; there was to be no compulsion on these latter to answer any further questions of mine; those on the record were to be sufficient. This, in itself, I think is a fair proof that in prosecuting my father's murderer I have acted with fairness and justice. If the slaves deny or disagree, then let the torture compel them to reveal the facts; for even if they have prepared a false tale, torture will soon force from them a true charge. I, for my part, know well that if the defendants had come to me, as soon as they heard that I meant to prosecute my father's murderer, and had offered to hand their slaves over to me, and I had refused to accept them, they would have used that as a convincing proof that they are not amenable to this charge. As it is, here I am: I am willing in the first place to apply the question myself and, on the other hand, I have urged them to do so themselves in my place: therefore it is only reasonable that these facts should be held as evidence of their guilt. If they had been willing to surrender the slaves for torture, and I had refused, they would have counted that as a point in their favour. Let me, then, now enjoy the same presumption, seeing that I was willing to put matters to a decisive test, and it was they who objected. It seems to me a strange thing that they should now try to persuade you not to condemn them, while they themselves did not think proper to give judgment in their own case by surrendering their slaves to torture. As far as that is concerned, it is very plain that they shrank from discovering the plain truth, knowing well that the crime, if revealed, would be found to concern them too nearly, and preferring therefore to leave it in obscurity without any further investigation. You, gentlemen, I am sure, will take the opposite course, and will let in the light of day. So much for that. I will now endeavour to give you a true account of what actually happened. May Justice guide me on my course.

In our house there was an upper room which was occupied by one of my father's friends, a man of position and repute, named Philoneos, whenever he was staying in town. Now

Philoneos had a concubine whom he proposed to sell into a brothel, and my brother's mother, hearing of her, made the girl's acquaintance. Later on, when she learned of the wrong that Philoneos was going to do, she sent for her, and on her arrival told her that she also was being misused by my father. "If you will do as I bid you," she said, "I will win you back Philoneos as a lover, and recover my own husband as well. I will devise the means, and you shall be the instrument." She then asked if she was prepared to help, and the girl, without much hesitation, I imagine, promised her assistance. The next stage in the affair was this. Philoneos had a sacrifice to make to his household god at the Piraeus, while my father was at that moment preparing to sail for Naxos. It seemed, therefore, to Philoneos an excellent opportunity at one and the same time to escort his friend as far as the Piraeus, and after the sacrifice to entertain him there to dinner. His concubine came with them to help with the sacrifice, and when they reached the Piraeus, it took place without further incidents. When the ceremony was over, the girl began to consider how she should administer the potion to them, before or after dinner, and, on reflection, decided it would be better to give it after the meal, following therein the injunctions of that Clytemnestra, the defendants' mother. To relate all the incidents of that repast would be a story too long for me to tell and too long for you to hear. I will endeavour merely to give you a brief account of how the potion was actually administered. The two friends partook of a good dinner, as you can imagine, the host having a sacrifice to offer to the god of his household, and the guest being on the eve of a sea voyage. When they had finished, they made a libation and added hereto some grains of incense. But while they were murmuring their ineffectual prayer, the concubine slipped the poison into the wine she was pouring out for them; and furthermore, thinking that she was doing something clever, she gave Philoneos an extra dose, supposing that the more she gave, the warmer would be his love for her. She did not know then that she had been deceived by my step-mother, and suspected nothing until she was actually in her toils. For my father, she poured in a smaller amount of the poison. The friends having finished the libation, took in their hands the deadly cup—and drank their last draught on earth. Philoneos immediately fell down dead. My father lingered on in suffering for a time, and died three weeks later. The girl who was the tool and agent in this crime, although she was not primarily responsible, has already received the reward that she deserved: she was handed over to the public executioner to be broken on the wheel. Now—if you and heaven so will it—it is the turn of the woman who is the chief criminal and devised the whole scheme.

Consider then, gentlemen, how much more justice you will find in my plea than in my brother's. I call upon you to avenge the dead man whose wrongs must endure now through eternity. My brother will make no appeal for the dead, worthy though he be of pity and help and vengeance at your hands, impiously and dishonourably driven from life before his allotted hour by those who should have loved him most; he will rather make petition for the murderess, a petition impious and unlawful, which neither heaven nor you can listen to or grant, asking you to acquit her of a crime from which she herself refused to shrink. Assist, not the murderers, but those who were by premeditation slain, and that, too, by their nearest and their dearest. It rests with you now to come to a right decision, and that I am sure you will do. He will entreat you on behalf of his mother who is still alive, and who in her mad wickedness killed my father; and if he can persuade you, will ask that she escape punishment for her crime. I, on the other hand, in the name of my dead father, demand from you that she be punished in every possible way. You were called here and appointed as judges, in order that wrong-doers might pay the penalty. I have set the whole story before you that she may be punished for her sin, and I champion the cause of our father and your laws: wherefore I deserve your assistance, if I speak the truth. My brother, on the other hand, has come forward to aid this woman, in order that she may escape punishment for her crime and contempt of the law. Which deserves the more compassion, pray, the dead man or the murderess? The dead man, I imagine. In the eyes of gods and men that would be regarded as just and pious. I claim, therefore, that as this woman in her ruthless cruelty murdered my father, so she shall herself now be put to death by you and by Justice. She of her own accord plotted his death and slew him; he met an involuntary and violent end. The violence, indeed, is manifest, gentlemen. He was just going to sail from Athens and had been dining with his friend. She sent the poison, and gave instructions that it should be handed to him to drink, and thereby she brought about our father's death. How then does she deserve pity or compassion from you or from any man? She did not deign to pity her own husband, but devised against him an impious and shameful murder. Compassion, remember, is more appropriate in the case of involuntary outbreaks than it is when the crime is voluntary and the offence premeditated. As she killed him without shame or fear of gods, heroes, and men, so now she herself should be put to death by you and by Justice. If she meets with neither compassion nor pity nor regard from you, she will obtain the punishment that she most justly deserves.

I marvel myself at my brother's audacity, and at the state of mind that induced him to swear solemnly, on his mother's behalf, that he was quite certain she had no hand in this.

How can a man be certain when he was not there? Those who are plotting murder against their kin do not rehearse the details of their crime before witnesses, I imagine: they work in the dark, and as far as possible allow no one to know of their schemes. And until the fatal moment comes, when they see death staring them in the face, their victims are as ignorant as all the world. It is at that last instant, if they have the time and strength, that they call upon their friends and kinsmen, and take them as witnesses of the crime, and tell them the murderer's name, and enjoin upon them the task of avenging their injuries. That was the injunction my father laid upon me, when he was writhing on his last bed of sickness. If they cannot reach their friends, they put down the facts in writing and call their servants as witnesses, and tell them who is responsible for their death. I was only a child then, but it was to me rather than to his slaves that my father gave this information and command.

I have told my tale and rendered what help I could to the dead man and to the law. It rests with you, gentlemen, now to consider with yourselves the truth and to give a just verdict. And methinks the gods below who have received this injury will not be indifferent.

LYSIAS

De Caede Eratosthenis.

The speech "In defence of the killing of Eratosthenes" deals with life in an Athenian household of the lower middle class. Euphiletos, for whom Lysias writes, is accused of murder, and his answer to the charge is that his action was justifiable homicide, for the law of Athens allows a husband to kill a lover caught with his wife *flagrante delicto* under his own roof. The prosecution had alleged that Eratosthenes was not in the house of his own free will, but had been beguiled or even dragged in from the street, and murdered at the hearth altar where he had taken refuge. Euphiletos accordingly gives the court his version of the circumstances, and calls as witnesses the friends who assisted at the discovery of the guilty pair. His case, however, depends very largely on the credibility of the one female slave, who apparently formed his entire household.

I should esteem it a great advantage, gentlemen of the jury, if I were sure that in dealing with this matter you would give for me the same verdict as you would give for yourselves, if you were in my place: for well I know that if you feel for your neighbours as you feel for yourselves, there is not a man among you who will not be indignant at what has been done, and everyone of you will consider that any penalty is slight for people who pursue such ways as these. This would not be only your own personal judgment; it is the judgment of all Greece. In regard to this offence alone is the same punishment assigned in oligarchic and in democratic states, so that the weakest here stand on the same level with the strongest, and the meanest man is the equal of the most noble citizen. So particularly monstrous does all mankind consider this injury to be.

As regards the severity of the punishment, I imagine you all have the same ideas, and no one of you is so indifferent or careless as to think that indulgence in these matters is proper, or that those who are guilty of such conduct deserve only a trifling penalty. It is my task now, gentlemen, I consider, to prove to you that Eratosthenes debauched my wife and committed adultery with her; that he thereby brought disgrace upon my children and acted with insolent violence to me by entering my house; and that, finally, there has been no ground of enmity, save this, between him and me, nor was my action due to money considerations or hope of gain. I did not wish to make a profit; I only wanted my legal revenge.

I propose then, gentlemen, to tell you the whole story from the beginning, keeping to the plain facts and omitting nothing. My one sure chance of acquittal, I consider, is to put before you, if I can, all that has occurred.

When I decided to marry, men of Athens, and brought a wife into my house, I made this my rule of behaviour. I did not annoy her with excessive vigilance, but on the other hand, I did not leave her too much her own mistress to do whatever she pleased. I kept as close a guard over her as was possible, and took all reasonable care. After some time, a child was born, and then I began to feel confidence, and handed over to her the care of all my goods, deeming that to be the surest bond of union between us. At first, gentlemen, she was the best of women, a clever and thrifty housewife, exact in all her affairs. Then my mother died, and her death has been the cause of all my troubles. My wife went to the funeral: that fellow saw her walking in the funeral procession and after a time succeeded in corrupting her. He watched the maid who goes to do our marketing, made a proposal to her, and soon effected his purpose of seduction. I must tell you, gentlemen, that my humble home is built in two storeys, the upper part similar in style to my ground-floor, one containing the women's apartments, the other the men's rooms. Now when our baby was born, the mother began by nursing it herself, and to avoid any risk on the stairs at bath-time, I took up my quarters in the upper rooms, and the women came down to the ground-floor. Moreover, we soon got into the way of my wife leaving me to go and sleep with the baby downstairs, so that she might give him the breast and prevent him crying. This went on for a long time, and I never suspected anything. Such an arrant simpleton was I, that I thought my wife the most virtuous woman in Athens. Well, gentlemen, time passed away, and one day I came back home unexpectedly from the country. After dinner the baby began to cry and make itself un- pleasant: the maid was hurting it on purpose to cause a disturbance, as I heard afterwards; for the fellow was in the house. I told my wife to go and give it the breast to stop its crying, but at first she would not go: she pretended that she was so delighted to see me after my long absence. Finally, when I began to get angry and bade her be off: "Ah," she said, "you want to stay here and make love to the maid. I caught you pulling her about the other day when you were drunk." At that I smiled, and she got up and went away, pulling the door to in pretended jest and taking the key. I did not think anything of that, nor had I any suspicions; indeed, I soon fell asleep, for I had just come from the country and was glad to get to bed. It was drawing on for daybreak when she returned and opened the door. I asked her why the doors had been banging in the night and she pretended that the child's lamp had blown out, and she had gone next door to get a light. I said nothing, and believed her tale. I did, however, notice that her face was covered with powder —although her brother had not been dead a month—but still I said nothing about her conduct. I went out and left the house in silence.

Some time elapsed after these events, gentlemen, and I had no inkling of my misfortune, when one day an old person

came up to me. She was sent, as I heard afterwards, by
another woman that fellow had seduced and abandoned,
who, in her rage and indignation, had spied on him until
she found out the reason of his desertion. Well, the old lady
came to me, near my house, where she was watching, and,
"Euphiletos," said she, "don't think that I have come in
any spirit of officious interference: the man who is wronging
you and your wife happens to be an enemy of mine. If you
take the maid who goes to market and does your errands,
and torture her, you will discover everything. The man is
Eratosthenes, of Oea; he is responsible for this; he has seduced
your wife and many other women besides: that is his trade."

With that, gentlemen, she went off, leaving me in a state
of absolute bewilderment. All sorts of things came back to
my mind, which was soon teeming with suspicions. I re-
flected how I had been locked up in my rooms; I remembered
how that night both the yard-door and the street-door had
banged; and I thought again how my wife had powdered her
face. All this, as I say, recurred to me and I was full of
secret uneasiness.

Finally I went home, and bidding the servant-girl come
with me to market, I took her to the house of one of my
friends. There I told her that I had discovered all that was
going on in my house. "For you," I said, "there is the choice
of two alternatives. Either you will be whipped and sent to
the treadmill to pass the rest of your life there in misery;
or else you will tell me the whole truth, and I will then
pardon your offence and let you go unpunished. I want no
lies; just the plain truth."

At first the girl stood out. "You may do what you like,"
she cried; "I know nothing." But when I mentioned the
name of Eratosthenes to her, and told her that he was the
fellow who had been frequenting my wife's society, she got
frightened and thought that I had full knowledge of every-

thing. So at last she fell at my knees, and after I had assured
her that she should come to no harm, she laid definite information before me. She told me how the fellow after the funeral
had begun by accosting her, and how she had ended by acting as go-between, and how her mistress at last had been
persuaded. She told me, too, how my wife arranged their
interviews, and how at the women's festival she had gone with
his mother to the temple of Demeter, while I was in the
country. In fact she gave me exact details of all that had
happened.

When she had finished her tale, I said to her: " Take
care that not a soul on earth knows of this, or else my promises
to you will not stand. I want you now to give me visual
evidence. If your tale is true, I need no more words: I must
catch him in the act." She agreed to this; and a space of four
or five days elapsed. I will give you trustworthy proof of all
this later, gentlemen; but I should like first to tell you of
what happened on the last day. Sostratus is an intimate friend
of mine, and meeting him just after sunset on his way back
from the country, and knowing at that hour he would not
find any of his acquaintance at home, I invited him to dine
with me. We went, therefore, to my house and mounting to
the upper storey had dinner together: when he was sufficiently
refreshed he took his departure and I went to bed. While
I was asleep, gentlemen, Eratosthenes effected his entrance
and I was awakened by the servant-girl's whisper: "He's
here." I bade her look to the door, and creeping downstairs
quietly, left the house and went to this one and that of my
friends. Some I discovered were out, others on a journey;
but I got together as many as I could find, and obtaining
some torches from the nearest shops we made our way into
my house, the house-door having already been set open for us
by the girl. Then we forced the door of my wife's room,
and those of us who entered first saw him actually lying

with my wife, while those who came in later saw him standing naked on her bed. I myself, gentlemen, brought him to the ground with a blow on the head, and after twisting his arms behind his back and tying them with a rope, I asked him why he had thus wantonly outraged my household. He, for his part, acknowledged his transgression, and begged and besought me not to kill him, but to accept compensation in money. To that I made this answer: "It is not I who shall kill you, but rather the law of our state, which you have now transgressed. You preferred to it the indulgence of your lusts, and chose to sin thus grievously against my wife and against my children rather than to obey the laws and to conform to their discipline."

It was in these circumstances, gentlemen, that the fellow met the fate which the laws ordain for those who follow in his path. He was not dragged into my house from the street, as the prosecution have alleged, nor did he take refuge at the house altar. That, indeed, was impossible; for he was knocked to the ground at once in the bedroom, and I tied his hands behind him. Moreover, there were too many people there for him to have made his escape, and he had no weapon, knife or stick, wherewith to defend himself. The fact is, gentlemen, as I imagine you also know, wrong-doers never will acknowledge that their enemies speak the truth, but with lying words and lying tricks they attempt to stir up the passions of their audience. I will now ask the clerk to read out the law.

(The law is read by the clerk of the court to the jury.)

He did not deny his guilt, gentlemen: he acknowledged his offence and begged and besought me not to kill him, and was prepared to make a money payment. I refused to accept the sum he proposed, thinking that the law of our state was here more effective, and I exacted that penalty

which you have regarded as most just and enacted for those
who follow in his ways. I will now call my witnesses.

(The witnesses give their evidence.)

Now please read the law inscribed upon the pillar of the
Areopagus.

(The law is read by the clerk.)

You have heard, gentlemen, the express instructions
given to the court of the Areopagus, whose ancestral privilege,
confirmed in our time, it is to judge all cases of murder:
they are not to condemn any man who, finding a lover with
his wife, takes summary vengeance upon him. And so strongly
did our lawgiver appreciate the justice of this provision
with regard to lawfully married wives, that he imposed the
same penalty in the case of the less valuable class of concubines. Plainly, if there had been any penalty more severe
than death, he would have imposed it upon the seducer of
a married woman. As it is, not being able to devise anything
more severe, he thought that the same punishment should
apply in the case of a concubine. Please read that law also.

(The law is read by the clerk.)

You have heard the provisions of the law, gentlemen.
It ordains that if a man assaults a freeborn adult or child,
he must pay twofold damages; and if he rapes a woman, in
whose case summary vengeance is permissible, he incurs
the same penalty. So strongly did our lawgiver feel, gentlemen, that those who use force deserve a milder punishment
than those who use persuasion. The latter he condemned
to death, the former he merely amerced in double damages.
Those who achieve their ends by violence, he considered,
are hated by their victims; those who use persuasion to cor-
rupt the mind that they make another man's wife more
their own creature than she is her husband's; the whole

household comes under their control; and it is uncertain to whom the children really belong, to the husband or the paramour. Therefore in this case he assigned the penalty of death.

Our laws then, gentlemen, have not only acquitted me already of wrong-doing, but have themselves bidden me to exact this punishment. It rests with you to say whether they shall remain in force or be regarded as negligible. I, for my part, consider that every state establishes a code of laws with this object: when we are in doubt we may consult the law and discover what it is our duty to do. The laws instruct people, who have been wronged as I have been, to exact the penalty which I have taken. I call upon you to show your agreement with those laws; for if you do not, you will make adultery so safe that even thieves will be encouraged to pretend they are engaged in amorous intrigues, knowing well that if they give that reason for their actions, and pretend that it was for this purpose they have entered another man's house, no one will lay hands upon them. Everyone will realise that the laws respecting adultery may be disregarded, and that the verdict of your courts, the strongest power in all the state, is the only thing they have to fear.

Consider the facts, gentlemen. The prosecution allege that I told the maid that day to go after the young man. I should have thought myself justified, gentlemen, in using any method to catch the man who had seduced my wife. If I had told her to fetch him while it was still a matter of words and nothing had actually occurred, I should have done amiss. But when he had completed his work and had on many occasions entered my house, I consider that I should have been acting rightly whatever means I employed to catch him. But please notice that even here the prosecutors are not speaking the truth, as you will easily see by the following considerations. As I told you before, gentlemen,

Sostratus is an intimate friend of mine. He met me about sunset on his return from the country, had dinner with me, and when he was sufficiently restored, left me and went away. Now, gentlemen, if that evening I had already had designs upon Eratosthenes, pray consider first whether it would have been more to my advantage to dine abroad, or to bring a friend home to dine with me, seeing that in this latter case that fellow would have had less confidence in entering my house. Secondly, which of these two things do you consider likely? Should I have let my guest go, and be left alone without assistance, or should I have asked him to stay and help me in taking vengeance on the adulterer? Thirdly, do you not think that I should have sent round word to my friends in the daytime and asked them to assemble at the nearest house, rather than have started running about in the night, as soon as I was informed, not knowing whom I should find indoors, and who would be out? Why, when I went to Harmodius and to some of the rest, I discovered they were travelling abroad—I did not know it—while others were away from home, and I had to get whom I could. If I had previous knowledge, do you not suppose that I should have procured assistance and told my friends, so as to make my entry in safety—how did I know that he had not a knife on him?—and to exact my vengeance in the presence of numerous witnesses? As it was, I knew nothing of what was going to happen that night, and I brought with me just those friends whom I could find. I will ask my witnesses to go into the box.

(The witnesses give their evidence.)

You have heard my witnesses, gentlemen. I must request you now with regard to this matter to consider with your-selves whether there has ever been any reason for enmity, save this, between myself and Eratosthenes. You will find

M

that there has been none. He has never blackmailed me, he has never tried to expel me from the city, he has never brought a case against me in the civil courts. He knew no guilty secret of mine which might have urged me to get rid of him in fear of discovery, nor had I any expectation of making money by my action. In fact, none of those reasons exist which usually impel a man to plot another's death. So far from there having ever been any offensive language, or drunken quarrel, or difference of any kind between us, till that night I had never set eyes on the fellow at all. Why should I have taken upon myself this risk, if I had not received the greatest of all wrongs at his hands? Why, moreover, should I have brought in witnesses to offend the gods, when I might have done the deed in secret, if I had wanted to kill him outside the law?

For myself, gentlemen, I consider that this is no private vengeance of my own; it was undertaken on behalf of the whole city. People of his sort, seeing what are the rewards set for these offences, will be less inclined to sin against their neighbours, if they see that you also are of this same view. In the other event, our best course will be to cancel the existing laws and to pass a new code, punishing severely those men who keep their wives under guard, and giving complete impunity to those who wish to sin against them. That would be much fairer than for citizens to be led into a trap, as they are now. Our laws command us to deal with an adulterer, if we catch him, according to our wishes; and then they leave the injured party in a more dangerous position than those men have to face, who unlawfully seduce another person's wife. I have obeyed the laws of our city, and I now am risking the loss of life, of property, and all that I possess.

ISAEUS

On the Estate of Ciron

ISAEUS.

The eleven speeches of Isaeus now extant are all concerned with cases of a disputed inheritance, such quarrels, owing to certain provisions of the Attic Law, being especially frequent in Athens. A marriage was only recognised as legal if both parties were Athenian citizens: children by a foreign wife were regarded as bastards, and could not inherit. But while elaborate precautions were taken for the registration of a man's sons in their father's *deme* and *phratria*, no such formalities were insisted upon with daughters, and in many cases a woman's citizenship was a thing difficult of exact and legal proof. It is on this point that the speech chiefly turns, and on the further question of a woman's position after her father's death, when she was inherited by the nearest male relative as an appendage to the property. The arguments show all Isaeus' usual subtlety, and for the delusive character of many of them the reader should consult the notes in Mr. Wyse's monumental edition.

IT is inevitable, gentlemen, that one should resent attempts like this, when people not only have the audacity to claim what does not belong to them, but also hope by their sophistries to sweep away legal rights. And that is what our opponents are attempting now to do. When our grandfather Ciron died he was not without issue; I and my brother are the sons of his legitimate daughter; but my adversaries claim the inheritance as being next-of-kin, and insult us by saying that we are not the sons of Ciron's daughter, and that he never had a daughter at all. The motive of their action is purely their own covetousness and the size of the estate that Ciron left behind him, which they have taken by force and now control. They impudently assert that he has left nothing, and in the same breath they lay claim to the property.

Do not imagine, however, that I am fighting this case against the claimant to the inheritance; my real adversary is Diocles of Phlya, nicknamed Orestes. He has suborned him to annoy us, endeavouring to keep us out of the money which our grandfather Ciron left at his death, and to bring us into this dangerous position, so that he may not have to pay any part of it over, if you are misled and believe the claimant's assertions. In the face of this chicanery it will be best for me to inform you of all the facts, so that you may have full and complete knowledge of every detail in the case before you pronounce your verdict. If ever you have given your most careful attention to any suit, I implore you to give it to this to-day. It is only right that you should. There have been many lawsuits before this in Athens, but you will find that no set of persons have ever made a more impudent or barefaced claim to other people's property than these men are now doing. It is a parlous task for one utterly without experience of the courts to contend against artful oratory and lying witnesses; but I have high hopes that I shall obtain justice from you and that my powers of speech will be adequate for the statement of my rightful claims, unless perchance some such thing occur as I have reason to apprehend. I beg you then, gentlemen, to give me your kind attention, and if you think that I have been wronged, to render me such assistance as is just.

I propose then, firstly, to prove to you that my mother was Ciron's legitimate daughter. With regard to things that happened in the far past I shall rely on reported statements heard by witnesses; for those within our own memory, I shall put in the evidence of people who know the facts, as well as certain substantive proofs which are stronger than any depositions can be. When I have so far established my case, I shall then show you that we have a better right than the defendants to inherit Ciron's estate. I shall start from the same point as my opponents, and from thence onwards endeavour to instruct you in the real facts.

My grandfather Ciron, gentlemen, married his first cousin, my grandmother, she being the daughter of his mother's sister. After a short married life of four years she died, leaving one daughter, my mother. My grandfather, having only this one child, married his second wife, the sister of Diocles, and by her had two sons. My mother he brought up with his wife and her children, and in their lifetime, when she came to marriageable age, he gave her in wedlock to Nausimenes of Cholargus, bestowing upon her a dowry of one hundred pounds, together with a trousseau and jewellery. Three or four years later her husband fell sick and died, before my mother had borne him any children. My grandfather took her back to his house, but failed to recover her dowry from Nausimenes' estate, owing to the embarrassed condition of his affairs. Finally, he arranged a second marriage for her with my father, giving this time a dowry of forty pounds.

In face of the charges now brought by our adversaries, how would it be possible to explain the situation clearly? I looked about and found a way. It is absolutely certain that Ciron's house-servants and waiting-women must know whether my mother was or was not his daughter; whether she lived or did not live with him; whether he did or did not twice give a bridal feast to celebrate her marriage. They know also what dowry each of her two husbands received. Wishing then to supplement the evidence of my witnesses by examining them under torture, and thinking that you would put more trust in their statements when they had submitted to examination than you would if the examination was still to come, I called upon my opponents to surrender these slaves, men and women, to be questioned on these points and on all others wherewith they might be acquainted.

From the test of torture, however, this fellow shrank then, although now he will expect you to believe his witnesses. Yet if I can show that he refused, what alternative is there to the presumption that their evidence now is false, seeing that he has been unwilling to accept so convincing a method? Obviously there is none. To prove the truth of my statements, take first this deposition and read it aloud.

(The testimony of the witnesses present, when the challenge was made and declined, is read in court.)

Both in your public and in your private capacity, gentlemen, you consider that torture is the surest test of truth. When slaves and freemen are both available, and it is necessary to clear up a disputed point, you do not rely on the evidence of the freemen, but rather put the slaves to the torture, and seek thus to discover the real facts. In this you act reasonably; for you know well that while some witnesses have been suspected of giving false evidence, no slaves thus examined have ever been proved to have committed perjury under the rack. Will this fellow who shirked so sure a test want you now in his utter shamelessness to believe his false witnesses and invented arguments? It is not so with us. We wanted the evidence that was to be given to be put to the proof of torture; our opponents refused our challenge. So, in our opinion, it rests with you to believe our witnesses. Take their depositions, please, and read them to the jury.

(Evidence relating to the past history of Ciron's family is read.)

Who may be reasonably expected to know about the events of the past? Obviously those persons who were acquainted with my grandfather. Well, they have testified to what they were told. Who must know about my mother's marriage? The parties to the marriage contract, and those who were present at the ceremony. Well, the relatives, both of Nausimenes and of my father, have given evidence. Who know that my mother was brought up in Ciron's house, and was his legitimate daughter? The present claimants give clear evidence that this is true by their action in shirking the test of examination. You cannot reasonably then disbelieve our witnesses, while to theirs you can hardly give credence.

Besides, we can bring other proofs to show you that our mother was Ciron's daughter. He treated us as he naturally would treat his daughter's children; he never offered sacrifice without our being there: whether it were great or small, we were always present and joined in the proceedings. Not only were we invited on such occasions, but he always took us to the rural Dionysia, and we watched the sport with him, sitting at his side; and every festive celebration we kept in his company. When he sacrificed to his household god, a sacrifice which he thought of the highest importance, never introducing slaves or freemen outside his family, but doing everything himself, we used to take our part: we helped him to handle the offerings; we helped him to lay them on the altar; we helped him in everything; and as a grandfather should, he prayed the god to give us " Health and Wealth." Now if he had not considered us his daughter's sons, if he had not seen in us the only descendants left to him, he would never have done any of these things, but would have kept this fellow close to him, who now pretends to be his nephew. The truth of these facts is known most definitely by my grandfather's servants, whom my opponent refused to surrender for examination. But with the less recondite parts of my story some of my grandfather's friends are quite familiar, and their evidence I will now produce. Take their depositions, please, and read them.

(The evidence of Ciron's friends is read.)

This is not the only proof that our mother was Ciron's

legitimate daughter. It is shown also by our father's conduct, and by the judgment of the married women of our deme. When he married, our father gave a wedding-feast to which he invited his relations and three of his friends, and he presented the usual marriage-offering to the members of his phratria. Later on, the women of the deme selected our mother to be joint president of the Thesmophoria, together with the wife of Diocles of Pithus, and with her to perform the usual ceremonies. When we were born, our father introduced us into his phratria, taking the legal oath that we were the children of an Athenian woman lawfully betrothed. And although there were many members of the phratria, and they always looked very carefully to such points, no one made any objection or disputed the truth of his statement. If our mother had been what our opponents say she was, you must not imagine that our father would have given a wedding-feast and made a marriage-offering; he would rather have kept the whole business secret. Nor would the wives of the other demesmen have chosen her with the wife of Diocles to make sacrifice and preside at the holy ceremony; they would have entrusted the duty to some other person. Finally, the members of our phratria would not have accepted us; they would have charged our father with falsehood, and proved him guilty, if it had not been universally acknowledged that our mother was Ciron's legitimate daughter. The facts, indeed, were plain, and so many people were acquainted with them, that no objection was ever raised by anyone. Please call my witnesses now, who will prove the truth of these statements.

(Witnesses testify to the marriage ceremonies and the enrolment in the *phratria*.)

Furthermore, gentlemen, the conduct of Diocles after our grandfather's death shows plainly that we were then acknowledged to be the sons of Ciron's daughter. I came to fetch the body, intending to conduct the funeral from my own house, bringing with me one of my kinsmen, my father's first cousin. Diocles was not at home when I arrived, and having bearers with me I was prepared to take the corpse away. My grandfather's wife, however, begged that the funeral should take place from that house, and said that she wished to help us in laying-out and dressing the body, so that finally, gentlemen, I yielded to her tears and entreaties, and going to Diocles told him, in the presence of witnesses, that I would conduct the funeral 'from Ciron's house, that being his sister's earnest request. To that Diocles not only made no objection, but actually told me that he had already bought some things for the funeral, and given security for others, and asked me to repay him, agreeing to give me a receipt for the articles already purchased, and to introduce to me the persons who had received the earnest-money. He then casually let fall the remark, without my having mentioned the matter, that Ciron had not left a penny. Now, if I had not been Ciron's grandson, he would not have entered into these arrangements: he would have said: "Who are you? What right have you to bury him? I do not know you. You shall not enter the house." What he now has persuaded others to say he should have said himself. He said nothing of the sort, but asked me to bring him the money next morning. Call me my witnesses to prove the truth of these statements.

(Witnesses present at the interview with Diocles give their testimony.)

The present claimant to the estate followed Diocles' example of silence on that occasion, although he has now been induced by him to put in his claim. The next day, however, when I brought the money, Diocles refused to accept it, saying that my opponent had paid him the evening before. Still they allowed me to be present at the funeral, and I took part in all the burial rites, the expenses of the ceremony being paid neither by Diocles nor by my opponent, but being taken out of Ciron's estate. If I was not Ciron's grandson, my opponent ought not to have allowed me to take part in the funeral: he should have ejected me as an intruder. My situation in respect to him was not the same; I allowed him, as being Ciron's nephew, to join in the ceremony; but he should not have allowed me, if what they now have the impudence to say were true. At the time he was so dismayed by the real facts that he did not dare to open his mouth, or make any of his present impudent charges; even when at the grave-side I accused Diocles of robbing me of the estate and persuading him to put in his claim. Call me my witnesses to testify to the truth of this.

(Witnesses present at the burial give their evidence.)

From what source does a statement derive credibility? From the evidence that supports it, I imagine. And from what source do witnesses? From the tests, naturally, to which they can be put. Why should you disbelieve my opponents' pleas? Obviously, because they have shirked the trial of examination. How could anyone show more plainly that my mother was Ciron's legitimate daughter, than by using this method? With regard to the remote past, I produce witnesses who depose to what they have heard from men still living. I produce those who have personal acquaintance with the several facts and know that my mother was brought up in Ciron's house and regarded as his daughter, and that she was twice betrothed and twice given in marriage. My opponents, on the other hand, have shrunk from applying the test of torture to slaves who knew all the circumstances. By all the gods in heaven, I could not give you stronger guarantees than these, and I consider that those which I have mentioned are sufficient.

I will now show you that I have a better title to Ciron's property than my opponent. I think that as a general proposition it is already manifest to you that in respect of legal succession, collaterals do not come before descendants—how could they indeed? The first merely belong to the same family, while the others are of the same blood as the deceased. But since, in spite of that, my opponents have the audacity to claim the property, I will prove this point in detail from the laws. If my mother, Ciron's daughter, were now alive and Ciron had died intestate, and if my opponent were not Ciron's nephew, but his brother, he would be entitled to marry her, but not entitled to the property. If he had married her, the children born of the marriage would have been entitled to the property, when they came of age. So the laws ordain. If, then, in her lifetime the right to her property was vested not in him, but in her children, obviously the children she has left ought to inherit it, now that she is dead.

This is plain also from the law concerning maltreatment of parents. If my grandfather were alive, and in want, we, not his nephew, should be legally compelled to maintain him. The law ordains that a man shall maintain his ascendants; that is, his mother and father, his grandfather and grandmother, and his great-grandfather and great-grandmother, if they are alive. With these latter ties of kinship begin, and their property is handed on to their descendants. Therefore they must be maintained, even if they have nothing to leave. How then is it just that we should be liable for not maintaining our ascendants, when they leave nothing, and that our opponent should be heir to anything they happen to have left? That is obviously unfair.

I propose now to put one of the descendants, the first, against one of the collaterals, also the first, and then I will interrogate you on each case. That will be the easiest method of making things clear. Is Ciron's daughter or Ciron's brother nearer of kin? The daughter obviously. She is a descendant, he is a collateral. Are the daughter's children nearer or the brother? Plainly the children; they, too, are descendants—not collateral relations. If then we have such an advantage over the brother, much more do we rank before the nephew. I am afraid of wearying you by the repetition of acknowledged facts. You all inherit from fathers, grandfathers, and more distant ascendants without having to go to law to substantiate your claim. I doubt if anyone has ever been troubled before with such a suit as this. I will read you the law concerning maltreatment of parents, and will then try to explain to you the real object of these proceedings.

(The law is read aloud.)

Ciron possessed, gentlemen, a considerable estate. He had a farm at Phlya, easily worth two hundred and forty pounds. He also had two houses in Athens, one near the shrine of Dionysus in the Marshes, let to a tenant and valued at forty pounds; the other, in which he lived himself, worth ten pounds more. He also had some slaves, whom he let out on hire, two female servants, and a girl, who, with his house furniture, may be reckoned as worth another fifty. The total amount of his visible property amounts then to three hundred and forty pounds, and he had, beside, certain monies lent out at interest, from which he derived considerable sums. For a long time, indeed ever since the death of Ciron's sons, Diocles has been plotting, with his sister's help, to get possession of this estate. So, though she could have borne children by another husband, he did not arrange a divorce for her, fearing lest Ciron, if she left him, would take such measures as he should have done, regarding the disposal of his property. He persuaded her rather to stay on as his wife, and to pretend frequently that she was pregnant, and then to simulate a miscarriage, so that the old man might be kept continually hoping for children of his own, and not adopt either of us. Moreover, he was always slandering our father to Ciron, saying that he was plotting to get his money. As for the various debts owed to him and the interest due thereon, he persuaded him to call them all in, and to put into his hands the management of all his real property, beguiling the old man with flattery and sedulous attentions, until he got everything under his control. He knew that I should seek to be owner of all this property, since my grandfather had died, as being the nearest relative; but he could not prevent me from entering the house and attending to the corpse and staying there some time, for he was afraid to exasperate me too much. He preferred to suborn a rival claimant, promising him a fraction of the estate in the event of my defeat, although he really meant to take everything himself, and did not even acknowledge to my opponent that my grandfather had left any property, but pretended there was nothing. Directly after Ciron's death, having previously made preparations for the funeral, he asked me to pay him his expenses, as you have heard my witnesses testify, and then pretended to have received the money from my opponent and refused to accept it from me, thrusting me on one side in order that people might think it was he, and not I, who arranged my grandfather's funeral. But though he laid claim to the house and all the property, pretending that Ciron had left nothing, I did not think it right at such an unseasonable moment to use force and carry my grand-father's body away. My friends, indeed, advised me to do so, but I preferred to give them my assistance and take my part in the funeral, the expenses of which were defrayed from my grandfather's estate. I acted thus practically on compulsion; and so, in order that they might not take advantage of me by pretending in court that I had contributed nothing to the cost of the burial, I asked the advice of a religious expert, and on his instructions performed the ninth day rites in the most elaborate fashion at my own cost. Thereby I baffled their sacrilegious attempt and they cannot pretend that they paid for everything and I contributed nothing: I spent as much as they.

That is pretty well the real position, gentlemen, and these are the reasons why we have been so annoyed. When you realise the shamelessness of Diocles' life and his general method of behaviour, you will believe everything I have said. The wealth which supports his present magnificence is not his own. It was really the inheritance of his three half-sisters; but as their father died intestate, he foisted himself in as his adopted son. When two of the sisters, by their husbands, tried to get the money from him, he fraudulently got the husband of the elder woman shut up, and had him disfranchised; and though he was indicted for assault and battery, he has hitherto escaped punishment. As for the husband of the younger sister, he commissioned a slave to murder him, and then, getting rid of his tool, laid the responsibility upon her. He has, indeed, so frightened him with his abominable tricks, that he now has robbed him of his son and acts as guardian of the whole estate, taking the good land himself, and giving him some few pieces of stony ground. These people live in terror of him; but perhaps they might be willing to testify to the truth of these statements. If they will not, I will produce others who know the facts. Please call them first.

(Witnesses testify to the crimes of Diocles enumerated above.)

This man of violence and fraud has robbed his sisters of their property already; but still he is not satisfied. As he has escaped punishment for that crime, he comes here now to deprive us of our grandfather's estate. He has paid my opponent, I am informed, eight pounds as his share, and he is seeking to endanger our rights as citizens as well as our rights to this inheritance. If you should be so deceived by him as to think that our mother was not a citizen, then we are not citizens either; for we were born after the archonship of Eucleides. It is of no small thing, is it, that we see ourselves in peril? So long as our father and grandfather were alive, our birth was never challenged, nor our citizenship called in question. They are dead now, and henceforth, even if we win our case, we shall be exposed to taunts respecting our disputed origin—thanks to this accursed Orestes, who will surely come to a bad end. He was caught in adultery, and suffered the penalty appropriate to that offence; but he still carries on the game, as those who know his secrets testify. You have been told now the sort of person he is, and you will hear a more detailed account when we bring forward our indictment against him in person. I beg and beseech you now to shield me from insult and not to allow me to be robbed of the property that my grandfather left. Help me, each man of you, to the best of your ability. You have adequate proof from evidence, examination under torture, and law, that we are the sons of Ciron's legitimate daughter, and that we, as direct descendants, have a better title than our opponents to inherit our grandfather's estate. Remember the oaths which you swore before you took your seats, remember the story you have heard, remember the laws, and give your verdict according to justice.

I do not know that I need say more. I think you are now acquainted with all the facts. Please take the one remaining deposition, which proves that Diocles was taken in adultery, and read it to the court.

(The deposition is read.)

DEMOSTHENES

Against Conon

The speech against Conon was written for the plaintiff Ariston by Demosthenes. The facts are very simple, and familiar every day to our own police courts; a long-standing feud between neighbours, ending at last in an assault by one on the other, and subsequent proceedings at law. What gives the speech its interest is, firstly, the intense seriousness with which an Athenian regarded any infringement of his dignity or assault upon his person (Demosthenes himself, when slapped on the face by Meidias, argues passionately that his assailant deserves the death-penalty several times over); secondly, the rather lurid side-lights that the narrative throws upon the manners of a society whose rules of conduct were made by men for men.

I was assaulted, gentlemen of the jury, by Conon, the defendant in this case, and received such treatment at his hands that for a long time neither my relatives nor my medical attendants expected that I would survive. Contrary to their expectations I recovered and regained my strength; and I then brought this action against him for his insulting conduct. My friends and kinsmen, whom I consulted, told me that his behaviour rendered him liable to summary arrest for robbery, and to an indictment for assault and battery. But they strongly urged me not to undertake a task too great for my strength, or to appear as prosecutor in a charge unsuited to my age. Accordingly, I took their advice, gentlemen, and brought a civil action against him, although I should have been glad to have him tried for a capital offence. You will all excuse me, I am sure, for that, when you have heard what I have suffered, for, monstrous as was the assault he made upon me then, it is only on a par with his outrageous conduct afterwards. I beg you then all, as is only right, to lend a friendly ear to my account of my experiences, and then, if you consider that I have been injured and wrongfully treated, to give me my just redress. I will relate now the several incidents from the beginning, using as few words as possible.

Two years ago we went out to Panactus on garrison duty. The sons of the defendant Conon unfortunately were quartered in a tent near to ours: this was the cause of our original feud, and how we fell across one another you shall now hear. Every morning directly after breakfast they used to start drinking, and kept it up all day long, persisting in this conduct during the whole period we were in garrison. We, for our part, behaved abroad as we were accustomed to do at home. So, when the dinner-hour came for the company, these fellows would begin playing drunken tricks, usually on our attendants, but finally upon ourselves as well. They pretended, according to the occasion, that our slaves smoked them out with their cooking, or that they were abusive; and then they beat them, or emptied the chamber-pots over them, or made water on them, using every sort of wantonness and brutality. We noticed all this, but at first, in spite of our annoyance, we put it on one side. When they made a mock of us, however, and would not refrain, all the members of my mess—I took no separate action—went to the general and informed him of their conduct. He rated them soundly, not only for their outrageous insolence to us, but for their general behaviour in camp. Yet so far from ceasing or feeling ashamed, that very night, as soon as it got dark, they burst in upon us; and beginning with abuse they ended by striking me several times. They made such a turmoil and uproar round our tent that the general and his officers and some of the other soldiers appeared on the scene, and prevented us from suffering any serious hurt, or doing grievous harm to our drunken assailants. Things, however, had gone so far

N

that on our return home there existed, as you might expect, feelings of mutual enmity and resentment between us. Still I never thought of bringing an action against them or taking any notice of what had occurred: I simply made up my mind to avoid them for the future, and take care not to get into their company. It is my intention, firstly, to produce before you evidence of these statements, and then to relate my treatment at the defendant's hands. You will then see that, although it was his duty to rebuke his sons for their original misbehaviour, he himself has taken the initiative in conduct more monstrous still.

(Sworn depositions relating to the affair at Panactus are read.)

Such then are the acts which I thought it best to disregard Not long afterwards, one evening, while I was taking my usual walk in the market-place, in company with a man of my own age, Phanostratus of Cephisia, one of the defendant's sons, Ctesias, passed me near Pythodorus' place, close to the Leocorium. He was intoxicated, and seeing us he bawled out something, and then muttering unintelligibly to himself, like a drunken man, he went on up to Melita. There was a drinking-party here, as I heard afterwards, at the house of Pamphilus the fuller, the company consisting of the defendant Conon, a certain Theotimus, Archetiades, Spintharus son of Eubulus, Theogenes son of Andromenes, and a number of other fellows. Ctesias made them get up from table, and set off with them to the market-place. As it happened, we were returning from the temple of Persephone, and were strolling just close to the Leocorium again, when we fell in with their party. At the moment of collision one of them, a stranger, fell upon Phanostratus, and held him tight; the defendant Conon and his son and the son of Andromenes all grappled me. They began by stripping me of my cloak, and then they tripped me up and flung me into the mire, jumping on me and assaulting me with such violence that one of my lips was cut through and both my eyes closed. In this pitiful state they left me, unable to get up or to speak. As I was lying there I heard them using a lot of dreadful language. Most of it was just blasphemous, and I should shrink from repeating some of their words to you. One thing, however, which is evidence that the defendant was responsible for the assault, and clear proof that he devised the whole business, I will tell you. He began to crow, like a fighting cock who has won a main, and his friends cheered him on, calling out: "Use your elbows for wings and clap them against your sides." Later on I was carried home by some passers-by without my cloak; for these fellows had gone off with that. When they got to my door, my mother and the servant-maids began to shriek and bawl: with some difficulty they carried me to the public baths and washed me all over, and then showed the doctors my injuries. To prove the truth of these statements I will now call my witnesses.

(The evidence of the persons who carried the complainant home is taken.)

It happened, gentlemen, that a relation of mine, who is now in court, Euxitheus of Chollidae, and Meidias with him, were returning from a dinner-party, when they met me close to my home; they followed behind as I was carried to the bath-house; and they were present when the doctor was fetched. I was in such a weak state that, rather than carry me the long distance from the bath to my house, the company decided for that night to take me to Meidias'; and this was done. I will now ask the clerk to read their evidence, and you will see thereby that a number of persons know of the assault made upon me by these fellows.

(The evidence of Euxitheus and Meidias is read.)

Now please read the doctor's deposition.

(The doctor's evidence is read.)

The immediate result of the blows I received and the outrageous attacks made upon me was as I have just told you, and my account is testified by the evidence of all the persons who were actually eye - witnesses. Afterwards, although my doctor said he was not overmuch alarmed by my bruises and the swellings on my face, yet several attacks of fever ensued in succession, accompanied by violent and distressing pains all over my body, and especially in my abdomen and my side. I was cut off all food; and, as the doctor said, if a copious discharge of blood had not come of itself to relieve me, just when I was in extreme agony and danger, I should have died of suppuration. As it was, the loss of blood saved my life. That I am speaking the truth and that the result of their attack was an illness, which nearly had a fatal ending, will be proved by the evidence of my doctor and my attendants. Please read it.

(The evidence is read.)

That their assault was of no slight or trifling character, and that my life was endangered by the violence and outrageous conduct of these men, and that the proceedings I have now started are far more lenient than they deserve, is, I imagine, now abundantly clear to you. Perhaps, however, some of you are wondering what defence Conon will have the audacity to make to these charges. I will tell you, therefore, beforehand, the excuse which I am informed he has arranged to bring forward. He will try to divert your attention from the actual facts of the outrage, and turn the whole business into a humorous jest. He will tell you that there are many people in Athens, sons of men of rank and repute, who in youthful jocularity have invented for themselves nicknames, such as " The Stick-ups" and " The Self-oilers," and that they keep mistresses, and that his own son is one of their band, and that frequently blows are given and received

over a girl, and that you must expect such conduct from
young men. As for myself and my brothers, he will make
out that we are a violent, drunken set, vindictive, and without any decent feelings. I, for my part, gentlemen, bitter as
is my resentment for my wrongs, should be no less distressed, and think this second assault, if I may use the
expression, no less outrageous, if Conon were to seem to you
to be speaking the truth in this matter, and if you were so
lacking in judgment as to believe a man's statements about
himself or his neighbour's imputations, and not allow decent
folk the credit of their daily habits and way of life. We
have never been seen either drunk or acting violently, and
I do not think I am doing anything very unfeeling when
I demand legal redress for my wrongs. The sons of the
defendant, as far as I am concerned, may have as rigid and
as exuberant a member as they please; I merely pray to
heaven that they reap their due reward for describing themselves as they do. The rites into which these gentlemen
initiate each other are filthy and obscene, while their conduct
is such that decent folk are ashamed even to talk about it,
and much more to put it into practice.

But what have I to do with this? I should be very surprised to find that there is any excuse or pretence recognised
by a jury which will enable a man, convicted of assault and
battery, to get off scot-free. Our laws give a quite different
judgment. They have provided even against the excuse of
necessity carrying too much weight. For example: I have
been compelled by this fellow to make inquiries and look
into these matters—there are actions for evil-speaking: I
am told that their purpose is to prevent abusive language
leading on to mutual violence. There are actions also for
assault: they, I hear, exist in order that the weaker party
may not defend himself with a stone or the like, but wait
for legal redress. Indictments for wounding, again, are to

prevent wounds ending in murder. Even in the most trifling of all offences perhaps—abusive language—precautions have been taken to bar the last and most serious crime, that it may not end in murder, and men be led on insensibly from abuse to blows, from blows to wounds, from wounds to death. The penalty for each offence is left to the law and does not depend on the wish and temper of any chance individual. Such is the law.

If Conon then says: "We are a company of 'stiff uns,' and when we are after the girls, we knock down and throttle anyone we please"—will you laugh and let him go? I trow not. None of you would have felt like laughing, if you had been there, when I was dragged along, and stripped, and violently assaulted, and carried home disabled to the house which I had left in perfect health. My mother came flying out, and the women set up such a bawling and crying —just as though someone was dead—that the neighbours sent in to us to inquire what had happened. Speaking generally, gentlemen, no one should be allowed on any pretext to commit an assault and then go unpunished: but if any excuse is permissible, it should be reserved for youthful folly and then imply, not escape from penalty, but merely mitigation of sentence. But when a man more than fifty years of age, in company with younger men—and those his sons—not merely failed to hinder or prevent this outrage, but was himself the chief culprit, the ringleader, and the most filthy rascal of all the crew, what punishment can be adequate for his crime? Death itself, methinks, is not sufficient. Even if he had done nothing himself, but had only stood by while his son Ctesias was acting the part which I have shown you he played, even then he would incur your righteous indignation. If he has brought his sons up in such a fashion that they are now neither ashamed nor afraid in his presence to commit crimes, for some of which the penalty is death, what sentence, think you, does he not rightly deserve? I consider that this is proof that he had no respect for his own father. If he had feared and honoured him, he would claim a like regard from his own sons.

I will now ask the clerk to read you the laws relating to cases of assault and highway robbery. The defendants, you will observe, are amenable to both.

(The laws are read in court.)

Conon's conduct has rendered him liable to punishment under both these laws: he has committed an assault and also a highway robbery. And even if I have not chosen to take advantage of them, that merely proves my retiring and modest disposition; he is a rascal all the same. If anything had happened to me, he would have incurred a charge of murder and the most severe penalties. The father of the priestess at Brauron, who, admittedly, never touched the dead man, but merely encouraged his assailant to strike him, was exiled by the Court of Areopagus.

And rightly too. If bystanders, instead of preventing, encourage people under the influence of wine or anger or some other cause to do wrong, then there will be no hope of escape for those who come across these wanton knaves; they will be knocked about, as I was, until the others are tired.

I will now tell you what they did when the arbitration was taking place, whereby you will see the outrageous sort of conduct in which they indulge. They dragged out the proceedings till past midnight, refusing either to read the evidence or to put in copies. Each one of my witnesses they took to the altar and put them on their oath. They offered evidence that had nothing to do with the case; for instance—" This was his child by a mistress, and such and such things happened." I assure you, gentlemen, everyone present was filled with disgust and indignation; and at last they were disgusted with themselves. When they were tired and had their fill of these tricks, in order to prevent the record-boxes being sealed, they put in a delusive challenge, saying they would surrender certain named slaves to be examined as to the blows. On this point, I believe, most of their defence will turn. I think, however, you will all realise that if they had offered this challenge, purely to have the slaves examined, and relying upon that as a just method, they would not have offered it at night-time, just when the arbitration award was due, and when no other pretext was left them. They would have done so at the beginning, before the case was brought, while I was lying ill in bed, not knowing whether I should recover I told everyone then who visited me who it was that gave the first blow and was responsible for my most grievous injuries, and then it was that he should have come straight to my house with all his witnesses, offered to surrender his slaves, and summoned some members of the Areopagus to attend. If I had died, the case would have come before them. If he was ignorant of the facts, as he will now pretend, and, having this just plea, had not prepared to use it in the face of so great a danger; at any rate, after I had recovered and summoned him, he should have offered his slaves at the first meeting before the arbitrator. He did no such thing. Please read now this deposition, which proves both the truth of my statement and the delusive character of his challenge.

(Evidence as to the arbitration proceedings is put in and read.)

As regards the examination of the slaves, remember, pray, the time at which he made the challenge, his fraudulent purpose in so doing, and the first occasions, when it is obvious he had no desire for this test, and made neither claim nor challenge. Before the arbitrator he was convicted on all the points which I am proving now before you, and was clearly shown to be guilty on every count. Accordingly he put in false evidence, writing down as his witnesses men whose names I think you will know, when you hear them: " Diotimus son of Diotimus of Icaria, Archebiades son of Demoteles of Alaea, Chaeretimus son of Charimenes of Pitthus, testify that they were coming back from dinner with Conon, and found Ariston and Conon's son fighting in the market-place, and that Conon did not strike Ariston." He supposed, forsooth, that you would believe them at once, and would not consider the real facts; to begin with, that neither Lysistratus nor Paseas nor Niceratus nor Diodorus, who have formally testified that they saw me beaten by Conon and stripped of my cloak and assaulted in other ways, men who were strangers to me and accidentally witnessed the affair, would have thought of giving false evidence if they had not seen his brutal treatment of me; in the second place, that if he were not my assailant, I should not have let off men who are acknowledged by the defendants themselves to have struck me, and preferred to indict someone who never laid hands upon me at all. Why should I? The man who struck me first and most brutally assaulted me, against him my indignation is directed, and against him I bring this suit, which I mean to fight to the end.

   Such then is my case: it bears all the marks of truth, and it is indeed true. The defendant, if he had not these witnesses to bring forward, would not have had a leg to stand on and must have let the case go by default. They, who are his boon companions and partners in many similar pieces of mischief, naturally have given false evidence. If things are to go like this and truth is to be of no avail when fellows once cast off all shame and dare openly to testify to falsehoods, then indeed we are in a parlous state. " We are not men of that sort," perhaps they will say. I think, however, that many of you are acquainted with Diotimus and Archebiades and grey-haired Chaeretimus, fellows who in the daytime look severe, and pretend to love Spartan ways, and wear thick cloaks and light sandals; but when they get together by themselves go to any length of vice and debauchery. This is the fine manly way in which they talk: "Shall we not bear witness one for the other? Is not that the duty of friends and comrades? What charge can he bring against you that you need fear? Some people pretend they saw him beaten. We will take our oath that you never touched him at all. Stripped of his cloak, was he? They did it first. His lip stitched up? We will say your head or something else was broken." In my case, gentlemen, I produce medical evidence. They do not. They will find it hard to get any evidence against me, except what they furnish themselves. They are ready for anything, and it is really impossible for anyone to say to what lengths they will not go. I should like you, however, to know the sort of things they go about doing, and I will ask the usher to stop the water-clock while the clerk reads you these depositions.

(Evidence as to the doings of Conon's associates is read.)

Men who commit burglary and strike anyone they meet— do you think that they would hesitate to bear false-witness on a slip of paper for one another, fellows who are leagued together in brutality and vice and shamelessness and violence? These are the words, I think, that are properly applicable to their conduct. They have in truth committed worse offences than those whereof you have just heard; but I could not discover all the people who have received injury at their hands.

I think it well to warn you of one most impudent thing which I hear they intend to do. They say he means to bring his sons into court, and to swear on their heads with certain dreadful and violent imprecations, which a person who heard them with amazement has reported to me. Such audacity as his, gentlemen, is unbearable; for the most worthy of men who are themselves the least likely to tell an untruth are the most often deceived by these tricks. Look rather at his character and his manner of life before you give him credence. How little he recks of an oath's obligation I will tell you now, for I have had perforce to make inquiries into these matters. I am told, gentlemen, that a certain Bacchius, whom you condemned to death, and that blear-eyed fellow Aristocrates, and some others of the same sort, were close comrades of Conon's in their youth, and that they took the name then of " Mohocks." They were in the habit of eating the sacrificial meats, and used to collect the testicles of the pigs which are used for purification before an Assembly, and make of them a joint repast; while as for false oaths and perjury, they were for them the easiest things in the world. A man of Conon's stamp cannot be believed on his oath. Far from it. A person who would never take even a righteous oath in an irregular fashion and would always refuse, whatever he had suffered, to swear on his children's heads, although, if necessary, prepared to swear as the law directs; he is far more worthy of credence than one who swears by the altar's fire and upon his sons' lives. I then, who am on every count more deserving of belief than you are, Conon, consented to take this oath; not because I am ready to do anything, like you, to escape punishment for misdeeds, but in the name of truth, and to avoid further violence at your hands, without having recourse to perjury. Read please my challenge on oath.

(The sworn statement of Ariston, challenging Conon to disprove the charge of assault, is read.)

I consented then to take this oath, and now, gentlemen,

to satisfy you and all here present, I swear again by all the gods and goddesses that I really suffered at Conon's hands the injuries that form the subject of this case; that I was beaten by him, that my lip was cut so deeply that it had to be sewed up, and that I am bringing this suit because of the violence done to me. If I swear truly, may I prosper and never be treated thus again! If I am a perjurer, may I perish utterly, myself and everything that is now or may be mine! But I am no perjurer: even though Conon burst himself with spite. I beg you then, gentlemen, as I have put before you the justice of my case and have given you in addition the pledge of my oath, I beg you to show on my behalf against Conon the same indignation that each one of you could have felt in his own case. Do not suppose that my injuries are not your concern: they might be done to anyone. Whoever be the victim, give him your assistance and grant him redress. Show your detestation of these fellows who are bold and careless before the offence, shameless and good for nothing when called to account, caring naught for reputation, character, or anything, if only they escape punishment. Conon will use the language of supplication and tears. But consider which is the more worthy of pity; the man who has suffered what I have at his hands, if I leave the court beneath a fresh load of disgrace without redress; or Conon, if he is punished? Is it to your individual advantage to allow assault and battery or is it not? I imagine, not. If you let him off, there will be many others like him; if you punish him, fewer.

I could speak at length, gentlemen, about the services which I and my father in his lifetime rendered you: we fitted out a trireme, we served in the army, and we fulfilled all the duties laid upon us. And I could point out that the defendant and his sons have never done anything. But my allotted time is not sufficient for this, nor are these now the questions before you. Even if confessedly we were more worthless and contemptible than the defendants, even then, I imagine, we do not deserve to suffer assault and battery at their hands.

I do not know that I need say more; I imagine that you are now fully acquainted with the facts.

THEOPHRASTUS

The Characters

Theophrastus, who succeeded Aristotle as head of the Peripatetic School, was an observer of society as well as an observer of Nature. His most elaborate work is the *History of Plants*, but his little book of *Characters* is even more valuable to those who believe that the proper study of mankind is man. He writes when Athens was already in decadence and had ceased to be the political centre of the Greek world; but his period is not so far removed from the age of Pericles as to exhibit any important differences in social life. The types that Theophrastus describes give us a picture of the Athenian as he walked and talked and had his being; and for true observation and vivid realism, the picture can hardly be surpassed. In my version I have followed Jebb's numbering, and usually his text: my obligations to his notes and translation will be manifest.

1. *The Flatterer*

ONE may hold flattery to be a sort of association which, though degrading, is profitable to him who practises it.

The flatterer is the sort of person who as he walks by your side will say: " Do you realise how people turn their eyes towards you? This happens to no one in Athens except you. They were singing your praises yesterday in the Arcade. There were more than thirty of us sitting there, when the question was started: Who is our most worthy citizen? Everyone began with you, Sir, and ended, Sir, by coming back to your name." While he is talking like this, he will pick a morsel of fluff from his companion's cloak; and if the wind has blown a piece of chaff on to the other's hair, he will remove it, adding with a smile: " Do you see? Just because I have not met you for two days, your beard is full of white hairs; although no one has darker hair for his age than you." While his patron is speaking he will bid the company be silent, and will praise him in his hearing, and when he pauses, act as fugleman with a "Bravo!" If he makes a frigid joke, he will burst out laughing, and stuff his cloak into his mouth, as though otherwise unable to restrain his mirth. To people whom he meets he will call out: " Halt, until the great man has passed by." He will buy apples and pears for the children and bring them to the house and give them in the father's presence, saying, with a kiss, " Chicks of a noble sire." When he goes with his patron to the shoe-market to buy a pair of slippers, he will declare that the foot is more graceful than the shoe; and if he is visiting a friend he will hurry ahead and say, " He is coming to see you," and then, turning back, " I have announced your approach." He is quite capable of running full tilt to the women's market and doing commissions there. At a dinner-party he is the first to praise the wine, and from his place next to the host will say, " What delicious fare!" and, taking something from the table, " Really, how excellent this is!" He will then ask the host if he is not cold, and whether he would not like a wrap, and while he is speaking will put one carefully round him. Moreover, he will lean close to his ear and whisper, and while he is talking to other people will keep his eyes fixed on him. At the theatre he will take the cushions from the slave and put them in place with his own hands. He will say that his patron's house is the perfection of architecture, that his farm is a model of cultivation, and that his portrait is an exact likeness.

2. *The Bland Man*

Blandness may be defined as behaviour calculated to give pleasure, but not inspired by the best motives.

The bland man is just the sort of person who will hail you at a distance with " My dear fellow," and after a great show of admiration, will take you by both hands and refuse to let go. He will come with you a little way and ask, "When, dear sir, shall I see you again?" and finally, with one last compliment, tear himself away. If he is called upon to act as arbitrator in a lawsuit, he tries to please, not only his principal, but the other side as well, so as to seem quite impartial. He will say of strangers that they have more justice in their arguments than have his own fellow-citizens. When he is invited to dinner, he asks his host to call the children in; and when they appear, he says that they are more like their father than one fig is like another. Then he draws them towards him and kisses them and puts them on his seat; with some he will play games, singing: "Here comes the hatchet and here is the skin"; while others, to his extreme discomfort, he will allow to go to sleep upon his stomach

3. *The Morose Man*

Moroseness is discourtesy in words.

The morose man is one who when he is asked where so-and-so is, will say, "Don't bother me." When he is spoken to, he will not reply; and if he has something for sale he does not tell prospective purchasers what he will sell it for, but asks them, "What is it worth to you?" When people send him a complimentary gift of food for a festival dinner, he growls, "I never touch presents." If anyone by accident soils his cloak, or pushes against him, or treads upon his toes, he never forgives him. If a friend asks him for a subscription he will say "No"; but later on he will come with it and remark, "More money wasted!" When he stumbles in the street, he is apt to swear at the stone. He cannot abide waiting long for anyone, and he never is willing to sing or recite or dance. He is apt also not to say his prayers.

4. *The Arrogant Man*

Arrogance is a sort of contempt for everyone except oneself.

The arrogant man is the sort of person who will tell someone anxious for an interview that he will see him after dinner when he is taking his usual stroll. When he has rendered a service he always says, " Be sure and do not forget." He will decide an arbitration case for those who have put it in his hands, as he saunters along the street. When he is nominated to public office, he takes a formal oath that he cannot serve, alleging that he has not the time. He will never be the first to make advances to anyone. As for his tenants and people who have something to sell, he is very apt to bid them return to his house at daybreak. When he is walking in the streets he never chats with those he meets, but keeps his shoulders bent, or at other times, if it pleases him, struts with his head in the air. If he is entertaining friends, he does not dine with them himself, but tells an underling to look after them. When he intends to pay a visit, he sends someone in front to say that he is coming. He will never let anyone see him when he is anointing himself, or in his bath, or at dinner. He is extremely apt also, when he is reckoning an account with you, to bid his slave push the counters away and set down an arbitrary total. In writing a letter he does not say, " I should regard it as a favour," but " I wish it," or " I have sent my servants to you," or " See that this be exactly carried out," or " Without an instant's delay."

5. *The Cynical Man*

Cynicism may be roughly defined as an affectation for the worse in action and speech.

The cynic is the sort of man who insists on going up to

o

his enemies and chatting with them, instead of showing his dislike. He will praise to their faces people whom he has attacked behind their backs, and when they have been worsted in court will express his sympathy. He will excuse people who revile him, even when the insult is fresh, and will talk in a bland way to those who are smarting under an injustice. When persons wish to see him at once, he tells them to call another time. He will never acknowledge anything that he is doing; he says always that he is thinking about it. He will pretend, " I have only just arrived," or " I was too late," or " I have been unwell." To applicants for a loan or a subscription, his answer is " I have no money"; when he has anything for sale, he pretends that he is not a seller; and when he does not intend to sell, he ays that he does. Hearing, he will affect not to have heard; seeing, not to have seen; and if he has agreed to anything, he will pretend to forget. With him, it is now, " I will consider the matter," now " I am not sure," now " I am surprised," and now " That was just what I thought myself long ago." In general he is apt to use this sort of expression: "I do not believe it," "I do not understand it," ' I am quite bewildered." He will say: " I have heard that already from someone else: moreover, his account did not agree with yours," " It is a very strange story," " You need not tell *me* that," " I do not know how I can disbelieve you or condemn him," "Take care and do not be too credulous."

6. *The Boaster*

Boastfulness would seem to be exactly an affectation of unreal advantages.

The boaster is the sort of man who will stand on the quay and expatiate to strangers about the large sums of money he has on the sea: he will discourse of the importance of his money-lending business and the huge amounts he has made and lost; and, while he is giving this impression of wealth, he will send his boy to the bank, where he has one shilling on deposit. He is an adept at imposing upon a companion with tales of his campaigns with Alexander, and of how intimate he was with him, and of what a lot of jewelled cups he brought back home; arguing that craftsmen in Asia are more skilful than Europeans; and all the while he has never been out of Attica. He will declare that a letter has just reached him from Antipater—"this is the third I have had"—bidding him come to Macedonia; and that, though he was offered a concession to export timber free of duty, he declined it; "no one shall accuse me of being too friendly with the Macedonians." He will say, too, that in the famine he expended more than twelve hundred pounds in contributions to his distressed countrymen—"I can never say No"—and then, although the company are strangers to him, he will ask one of them to get out his counting-board, and reckoning by five pounds and fifties, and giving plausible names to each contribution, he will arrive at a total of two thousand four hundred pounds. "This," he will say, "was what I spent in charity: I am not counting the money that the galley cost me or my other public services." He will go into the horse-market, where the thoroughbreds are sold, and pretend that he is anxious to buy: or he will visit the upholsterer, and ask to see tapestries to the value of five hundred pounds, and then abuse his attendant for not having brought any gold with him. He lives in a hired house, but pretends to anyone who does not know him that it is the family mansion. "I mean to sell it, however; it is too small for my entertainments."

7. The Man of Petty Ambition

Petty ambition would appear to be a sordid craving for honour.

The man of petty ambition is the sort of person who, when asked to dinner, will make a great point of being placed next to his host at table. He will take his son to Delphi to have his hair cut. He will see to it that his page-boy be an Ethiopian, and when he pays money away, he will have his slave pay it in new coin. He will have his hair cut very often, and will keep his teeth white: he will change his clothes while they are still in good condition, and anoint himself with expensive unguent. In the market-place he will frequent the bankers' tables; he will be an habitué of those gymnasia where the young men exercise; and in the theatre, when there is a performance, he will sit near the generals. He never buys anything for himself; his purchases are commissions for acquaintances abroad—pickled olives to Byzantium, Spartan hounds to Cyzicus, honey from Hymettus to Rhodes; —and while he is thus engaged he will talk at large to his stay-at-home friends. He is very apt to keep a monkey; and among his other acquisitions will be a short-tailed ape, Sicilian doves, dice made of deer-horn, Thurian vases— the correct round shape—walking-sticks from Sparta properly curved, and a tapestry curtain with figures of Persians embroidered upon it. He will have also a little court for wrestling-matches strewn with sand, and a fives-court, and will go about and lend it to philosophers, lecturers, fencing-masters, and professional musicians for their performances: at which he himself will appear upon the scene rather late, so that the spectators may whisper one to the other, "That gentleman is the owner." When he has sacrificed an ox he will nail up the skin of the forehead and wreathe it with large garlands, that everyone who comes in may see that he has sacrificed an ox. When he has been riding in a procession of cavalry, he will give the rest of his equipment to his slave to carry home; but after putting on his ordinary cloak, he will stroll about the market-place in his spurs. He is apt also to buy a little ladder for the jackdaw he keeps indoors, and to make a little brass shield for the jackdaw to hold as it hops up the ladder. If his little Melitean dog dies, he has a grave made with a pillar inscribed: "Klados of Melita." If he has made a votive offering of a brass ring in the temple of Asclepius, he will wear it to a thread with his daily oiling and polishing. It is just his way to make a special arrangement with the presidents of the Council, whereby he shall report to the people the result of the sacrifices. He provides himself with a fine new cloak and a wreath, and coming forward says: " Men of Athens, we, the presidents, have been sacrificing to the mother of the gods. The sacrifice has been auspicious and favourable. Receive ye now her good gifts." And after making this announcement he will go home and explain in detail to his wife how excessively fortunate he has been.

8. *The Late-Learner*

Late-learning would seem to be a laborious pursuit of knowledge unsuited to one's age.

The late-learner is a man who will commit to memory long speeches from a play when he is sixty years old, and then forget the words when he is reciting them at table. He will take lessons from his son in " Right turn," and " Left turn," and " About turn." At the festivals of heroes he will contend with the small boys in an impromptu torch-race; and it is very much his way, if he be ever invited to a temple of Heracles, to fling off his cloak and seize the ox in order to bend its neck back. He will go to the wrestling-school and indulge in a bout; at a show he will sit through three or four performances, trying to learn the songs by heart; and when he is being initiated into the rites of Sabazius, he will do his best to get special commendation from the priest.

He will ride to his farm on a borrowed nag and practise tricks of horsemanship on the way; and, falling off, will break his head. On a tenth-day feast he will get people together to join him in playing the flute. He will have a game of leap-frog with his footman, and compete at archery and javelin-throwing with his children's attendant, saying, "Learn from me," as though the other also knew nothing about it. At a public bath, when he is wrestling, he will make all sorts of feints and wriggles, to show how well he has been trained; and when women are near he will practise the steps of a dance, whistling his own accompaniment.

9. *The Unseasonable Man*

Unseasonableness consists in choosing a time for action which is annoying to your companion.

The unseasonable man is one who will go up to a busy person and start telling him all his affairs. He will serenade his lady-love when she has a fever. He will accost a man who has just been fined in a surety-suit and ask him to go bail for him. If he is to give evidence, he arrives in court after the verdict has been pronounced. When he is invited to a wedding-feast he inveighs against womankind. To those who have just returned from a long journey he proposes a stroll. He is very apt also to bring you a higher bidder when you have already concluded a sale. If people have heard all about a thing and know it by heart, he will get up and tell them every detail again. He loves to charge himself with services which you do not want, but are ashamed to refuse. When people are spending money on a sacrifice he will come to demand interest on money he has lent them. If a slave is being flogged and he is standing by, he will relate at length how a slave of his was once beaten in the same way—and hanged himself. If he is assisting at an arbitration, he will set both parties at loggerheads, even when they are anxious to come to terms. And when he is minded to dance, he will catch hold of another guest who is not yet drunk.

10. *The Officious Man*

Officiousness would seem to be actually a kindly presumption in word and deed.

The officious man is the sort of person who gets up at a meeting and undertakes to do things which he can never perform; and when an arrangement is acknowledged to be just, he will raise objections and be proved wrong. He will force the slave to mix more wine than the guests can finish: he will separate people fighting, even if he is not acquainted with them: he will undertake to show a short cut, and then lose his way completely. Moreover, he will go up to the general and ask him when he intends to offer battle and what will be the orders two days ahead. If the doctor has forbidden him to give his patient wine, he will say he wishes to try an experiment, and will drench the invalid with liquor. He will inscribe upon a dead woman's tombstone the names of her husband and father and mother, as well as her own, with the place of her birth, adding further, "These were all persons of repute." And when he is preparing to take an oath, he will say to the bystanders, "I have done this frequently before."

11. *The Unpleasant Man*

Unpleasantness may be defined as behaviour that causes annoyance without doing any actual harm.

The unpleasant man is the sort of person who will come in and wake someone who has just gone to sleep, in order to have a chat. When people are just putting out to sea he will stop them, and running up beg them to wait until he has taken a stroll. He will lift his child from its nurse's arms, and feed it from his own mouth and call it by pet names, "Papa's little rascal." He is apt also to ask in the presence of his relatives: "Tell me, mammy, what was the day of the month when you were brought to bed with me?" He will tell you that he has cistern water at his house, very cool, and that his garden produces an abundance of fresh vegetables, and that his cook is an expert at made dishes. "My place," he will remark, "is a public hostelry; always full of people: as for my friends, they are like the bottomless cask; I cannot fill them, do what I will." When he is entertaining a stranger he will show off his parasite's accomplishments to his guest; and over the wine will call out encouragingly that the amusement of the company has been provided for.

12. *The Offensive Man*

Offensiveness is a painful neglect of the person.

The offensive man is one who will stroll about the town when suffering from scrofula or skin disease or overgrown nails, and will remark airily, "These are hereditary complaints with us. My father had them, and my grandfather, and it is no easy matter to get yourself foisted into *our* family." He is very apt also to have ulcers on his legs, and sore places on his toes, and through lack of attention allows them to fester. The hair under his armpits is coarse and thick and spreads over his body; his teeth are black and decaying. These are the sort of things he does: He will blow his nose at table, cover himself with blood at a sacrifice, eject morsels from his mouth during a conversation, and belch in the very act of drinking. He will go to bed without having washed, and by using rancid oil in the bath produce skin irritation. He will go out into the market-place wearing a thick tunic and a very light cloak, which is one mass of stains.

13. *The Stupid Man*

Stupidity, if we would define it, is mental slowness in speech and action.

The stupid man is the sort of person who, after reckoning up a sum with his counters and setting down the total, asks the man next to him, "What does it come to?" When he is defendant in a lawsuit, and it is about to come on, he forgets all about it and goes off to his farm. When he goes to see the play he falls asleep and is left by himself in the theatre. When he has taken something up and put it away himself he will start looking for it and not be able to find it. If the death of a friend is announced to him, in order that he may assist at the laying-out of the body, with a downcast look and tears in his eyes he will say, "Heaven be praised!" He is very apt to bring witnesses when he is receiving payment of a debt; and in winter-time he will quarrel with his slave for not having bought cucumbers. He makes his children wrestle and run races until they are completely exhausted. If on his farm he cooks the lentil soup himself, he puts a double quantity of salt into the pot and makes it uneatable. When rain is falling, he will say, "Well, the smell from the sky is delicious" (when other people, of course, would say "from the earth"). And if he is asked, "How many corpses do you think have been carried out at the Sacred Gate?" he will answer, "I wish that you and I had as many."

14. *The Boor*

Boorishness would appear to be an ignorance of the rules of nice conduct.

The boor is the sort of man who will drink a cheese posset before he goes to Assembly, declaring that the thyme wherewith it is flavoured smells sweeter than any scent.

He wears shoes that are too large for his feet, and he converses in a loud voice. He distrusts his friends and relations, but communicates his most important secrets to his slaves, and gives the hired labourers working on his farm all the latest news from the Assembly. He will sit down with his cloak pulled up above his knee. At most things in the streets he shows neither surprise nor admiration; but when he sees a bull or a he-goat or a stallion ass, he stands still and gazes with all his eyes. He is apt to take things from the store-cupboard before dinner and eat them, and he mixes his liquor too strong. He will make love to his cook on the sly, and will then help her to grind the corn for all the household and himself. He will give the cattle their fodder while he is eating his breakfast, and he will answer the door in person, calling his dog and taking hold of his nose, with "This is the fellow who guards the house and everywhere." When he is paid money he will reject one coin, saying that it is too smooth, and will take another in its place. If he has lent his plough or a basket or a sickle or a bag, he will remember it the next night as he lies awake and come to ask for it back. On his way down to town he will ask the first man he meets the price of hides and salt-fish, and whether the Archon is celebrating the New Moon to-day; adding at once that he is going down to have his hair cut, and that on the one journey he intends to get some salt-fish from Archias' shop, as he goes past. He sings at the bath, and puts heavy nails in his shoes.

15. *The Shameless Man*

Shamelessness may be defined as disregard for one's reputation, due to a desire for base gain.

The shameless man is the sort of person who starts the day by going to someone whom he is already keeping out of money and borrowing some more from him. Then, after sacrificing to the gods, he will put the meat into the salt tub and go out to dine with a friend. There he will call up his page-boy and give him bread and meat from the table, saying in the hearing of all, " Enjoy yourself with that, my honourable friend." When he goes marketing he will remind the butcher of any services he may have rendered him, and, standing by the scales, will throw in, for preference, a piece of meat, or if not that, a bone for the soup. If he gets it, he is happy: if he does not, he snatches up a piece of tripe from the counter and goes off with a laugh. Moreover, he will buy seats at the theatre for foreign guests, and then go himself without paying his contribution; and on the next day bring his children as well and their attendant. When anyone gets a thing cheap, he will ask to have a share. He will go to another man's house and borrow barley or bran, and then will force the lenders to deliver it. He is apt, too, to go up to the cauldrons in the bath-house, and, dipping in the bucket, to souse the water over himself, in spite of the bath-man's cries; then he will say, " I have had my bath," and, as he goes away, " No thanks to you."

16. *The Reckless Man*

Recklessness is toleration of shameful acts and shameful words.

The reckless man is one who will take an oath for fun, who is proof against abuse and able to answer back, in character a low fellow, defiant of decency, and ready for anything, quite capable of dancing the cordax in a comic chorus when he is sober and without a mask. At shows he will pass along the row and collect the coppers, wrangling with those who have got their ticket and claim to see the performance without further payment. He is apt also to become an inn-keeper or a tax-collector: there is no trade too disreputable for him to refuse: he will be a crier, or a cook, or a professional gambler: he will neglect to maintain his mother, be summarily arrested for theft, and spend more time in prison than in his own house.

He would appear, too, to be one of those persons who call out and collect a crowd round them, ranting in a loud cracked voice and carrying on abusive conversations with their audience. Some come up, and others go away without hearing him out; some get the beginning of his tale, some a résumé, some only a fragment; and he never thinks proper to make this parade of his recklessness except when there is some public gathering. He is an expert also at lawsuits, whether as defendant or prosecutor; sometimes he will swear his ignorance of the charge, at other times he will appear in court with a box of papers in the folds of his cloak and bundles of documents clutched in both hands. He will not think it beneath him to have under his command all the costermongers of the market: he will lend them money for the asking, and charge them threepence per day interest on a shilling loan, going the round of the cook-shops, fishmongers, and salters, and thrusting into his cheek the proceeds of his trade.

17. The Gross Man

A definition of grossness offers no difficulty: it is obvious and offensive jocularity.

The gross man is the sort of person who will expose himself before free-born women in the street. He will go on applauding in the theatre when the rest of the audience are ceasing, and will hiss those actors who please everyone else in the house. He will go into the market at forenoon, and standing by the greengrocers' stalls will nibble their nuts and berries while he gossips with the vendors. He will call by name to a passer-by, though he does not know him well; and if he should see people in a hurry, he will cry "Stop." He will go up to a man who has lost an important case when he is leaving the court and say, " I congratulate you." He does his own marketing, and himself hires the flute-girls; moreover, he shows everyone he meets the provisions he has bought, and invites them to partake, explaining, as he stands at the door of a barber's or perfumer's shop, that he intends to get drunk. When his mother has gone out to consult a soothsayer, he will use evil words; and when people are offering prayer and pouring libations, he will drop his cup and laugh as though he had done something witty. When he is being played to, he will be the only person in the room to beat time with his hands and to whistle the tune; and will find fault with the flute-girl, asking her why she did not stop playing sooner. And when he wants to spit, he will spit across the table at the cup-bearer.

18. *The Garrulous Man*

Garrulity is indulgence in long and inconsiderate talk.

The garrulous man is one who will edge up close to a stranger on a seat and begin by singing the praises of his own wife. Then he will narrate at length a dream he had last night; and next give a minute catalogue of what he ate at dinner. Then, warming to his work, he will say that people to-day are much greater knaves than were the men of old, and will exclaim at the price of wheat on 'Change, and the number of foreigners in town. Then he will remark that the sea is navigable after the Dionysia; and that if Zeus would send more rain, things in the ground would get on better; and that he intends to do some farming next year; and how hard it is to make a living; and that Damippus set up a very large torch at the Mysteries; and "How many pillars are there in the Odeum?" and "Yesterday I took an emetic"; and "What is the day of the month to-day?" and that the Mysteries are in Boedromion, the Apaturia in Pyanepsion, and the rural Dionysia in Poseideon. Indeed, if you can stand him, he will never leave off.

19. *The Loquacious Man*

Loquacity, if you wish to define it, would appear to be an incontinence of talk.

The loquacious man is the sort of person who will cry out to anyone he meets, if a word is said to him, "You are talking nonsense; I know all about it; listen to me and you will hear the truth." In the middle of your reply he will put in, "You say that, do you?" "Don't forget the next point in the story"; "Thank you for reminding me"; "How useful a chat is!" "As I forgot to say"; "You have soon caught my drift!" "I have been waiting all this time to see if you would come to the same conclusion as myself." These and other such cues he makes for himself, so that you never get a moment's breathing-space. And when he has finished dealing with individual listeners, he is apt to swoop down upon knots of people standing together and to put them to flight in the middle of their business. He will go, indeed, into school-rooms and wrestling-grounds and hinder the boys from learning their lessons by all this talk with their trainers and teachers. And when people say they must go, he makes a point of escorting them and seeing them safe home. He will report the latest news from the Assembly as soon as he has heard it, and will describe at length the great forensic struggle that took place in the archonship of Aristophon, giving extracts also from the famous speech that he himself once made before the people. In the course of his story he will slip in the usual abuse of mob-government; so that his audience either lose the thread entirely, or fall asleep, or break away and leave him in mid-channel. On a jury he will prevent his colleagues from arriving at a verdict; at a theatre he will stop his neighbours from enjoying the play; at a dinner-party he will hinder the other guests from getting any food, saying, " It is hard for a loquacious soul to be silent; my tongue is too well-oiled; I can't hold it, even though you think me a greater chatterer than the swallows." He even lets his own children mock at him; for when at last they want to go to sleep, they call to him and say, " Papa, start talking to us, and then we shall fall asleep."

20. *The Inventor of News*

Newsmaking is the composition, at the inventor's pleasure, of fictitious sayings and doings.

The inventor of news is one who, meeting a friend, will immediately put on a grave look, and with a solemn smile will say, " Where do you come from, and what is your news? What fresh information have you about this affair?" And then he will repeat with a pretence of urgency, " Is there anything particularly recent? Certainly this is glorious tidings." Then, without letting you reply, he will go on, " What's that? You have heard nothing? I think that I can give you a feast of news." He always has some special source of information: a soldier in the army, or a slave belonging to Asteius the musician, or Lycon the contractor; unfortunately one can never actually lay hands upon these authorities. Quoting from them, he will tell you how Polyperchon and the king have won, and Cassander has been taken prisoner; and if you say to him, " Do you believe it?" he will answer, " It is being shouted about all over the town. The story is gaining ground every hour. All are agreed about the battle. Each account is the same." He will then remark that it has been a regular hash-up, and that the faces of the Government are good evidence; they are looking very different to-day. He tells you, too, that he has heard on the quiet that the authorities have a man hidden away indoors, who arrived five days ago from Macedonia, and knows everything. And in telling all this story, you can imagine how plausibly pathetic he is, with his " Poor Cassander! Unlucky fellow! Mark the hand of fate! Ah well, for all his greatness—!" Finally he will beg you to keep this most strictly to yourself; when he has already run up with the tale to everybody in town.

21. *The Evil-Speaker*

Evil-speaking is an inclination of the mind to put things in the worst light in talking of others.

The evil-speaker is a man who, when asked who so-and-so is, will set out his answer in true heraldic style. " I will begin with the gentleman's parentage. His father was originally called Sosias; but when he joined the army he took the name Sosistratus; and when he was enrolled in his deme he became Sosidemus. As for his mother, she is a noble lady of Thrace— at any rate, her pet name professionally is Crinocoraca— and they tell me that in her country, damsels of her sort are held in high respect. Our honourable friend himself, as might be expected from his parentage, is—a low rascal." He is quite capable, too, of saying to someone, " Of course; I know what you mean: you are not far wrong in what you have told our friends here and me. Those ladies catch hold of passers-by and drag them in from the street. In that house they earn their living on their backs. The common talk about them is well founded: they behave like animals in the road. In fine, they love to gossip with men, and they answer the front door themselves."

It is very much his way also, when others are speaking evil, to chime in: " I, too, hate the fellow more than I hate anyone; his face shows what a rascal he is, while as for his bascness—there's nothing to equal it. Here's a proof. Ever since their child was born, he only allows his wife three-pence a day for food; and she brought him a dowry of over a thousand pounds. He makes her wash, too, in cold water, even in the depth of winter." When he is sitting with others, he is apt to start talking about anyone who leaves the room; and if he gets an opportunity he will not even refrain from abusing his own relations. He will freely slander his friends and kinsmen and the dead, giving to his evil-speech the false names of "frankness," "democratic spirit," and "inde-pendence," and making it the chief pleasure of life.

22. *The Grumbler*

Grumbling is undue fault-finding with what is given you.

The grumbler is the sort of man who, when a friend has sent him a portion of a sacrificial feast, will say to the messenger: "You grudged me your soup and your miserable wine, or else you would have invited me to dinner." He will be indignant with Zeus, not for not raining, but for raining too late; and if he finds a purse on the road, he will say: "I have never found a buried treasure." When, after having begged the vendor to sell, he has bought a slave cheap, he mutters: "I wonder if this bargain of mine is sound in wind and limb." To the messenger of the good news: "A son is born to you," he will reply: "If you add that half my property has gone, you will be speaking the truth." When he wins a lawsuit by a unanimous verdict, he finds fault with his speech-writer for having omitted many of his strongest points. If his friends have raised a subscription for him, and you say "Cheer up!", "Cheer up, indeed!" he will

P

growl, " I shall have to pay everyone his money again, and be grateful to them besides for their charity."

23. *The Distrustful Man*

Distrustfulness is a presumption of universal fraud.

The distrustful man is the sort of person who will send one slave to market and then despatch another to inquire how much he paid. He will carry his money himself and sit down every furlong to count it. He will ask his wife in bed whether she has locked the wardrobe, and secured the plate-chest, and if the outside door has been bolted; and if she says "Yes," none the less he will get up naked from the blankets, and light the lamp, and run round with bare feet to inspect all these matters, and even then with difficulty get to sleep. When he claims interest from his debtors, he brings witnesses with him, so that they may not be able afterwards to repudiate the debt. When his cloak needs cleaning, he is apt to send it not to the best fuller, but to the fuller who can give the soundest security for its return. If anyone comes to ask the loan of some silver cups, he will much prefer to refuse; but if perchance it be a close friend or relation, he will all but assay the plate and weigh it, and insist on a security, before he can bring himself to lend. When his page-boy attends him abroad, he bids him walk in front, not behind, as a precaution against his running away in the street. If people have bought something from him and say: "Reckon up the total and put it down to my account. I am too busy to send you the money this instant," he will reply: "You need not worry. I will come with you now and stay with you until you find time to pay me."

24. *The Penurious Man*

Penuriousness is excessive thriftiness in money-matters. The penurious man is the sort of person who, before the month is out, will come to your house and ask for half his month's interest. At a club-dinner he counts how many cups of wine each man drinks, and of all the company he pours the smallest libation to Artemis. If a person has made a good bargain for him, when the account comes in he always says it is too much. When a slave breaks a jug or a plate, he deducts the value of it from his rations; and if his wife has dropped a threepenny-piece, he is capable of moving all the furniture, even the bedsteads and the wardrobes, and searching under the floor-boards. If he has anything for sale, he charges a price that leaves the purchaser no profit. He will not let anyone eat the figs in his garden, or walk across his land, or pick up a single olive or date from the ground; and every day he inspects his boundary-marks to see if they remain the same. He is fond of distraining for debt and of charging compound interest. When he is entertaining his fellow-demesmen, he cuts the meat into very thin slices before he serves them; and if he goes marketing, he comes home without having purchased anything. He will forbid his wife to lend salt, or a lamp-wick, or cummin, or marjoram, or barley grain, or garlands, or sacrificial cakes. " These trifles," says he, "tell up in the course of a year." In fine, you will always notice that penurious people's money-chest has a mouldy look and that the keys are rusty; that they themselves wear cloaks too short for their legs; that when they anoint themselves they use very small oil-flasks; that they have their hair cropped close; that they take off their shoes in the middle of the day; and that they insist with the fuller that their cloak shall have plenty of earth on it, to prevent it soon getting dirty.

25. The Mean Man

Meanness is an excessive indifference to honour where expense is concerned.

The mean man is the sort of person who, when he gains the victory in a dramatic contest, dedicates a wooden scroll to Dionysus, inscribing upon it only his own name. When voluntary contributions are being asked for in the Assembly, he will get up without saying anything and retire. At his daughter's marriage-feast he will sell all the meat of the sacrifice except the priest's portion, and will hire the waiters on the understanding that they find their own food. When he is paying for the upkeep of a galley, he will use the steersman's bedding on deck, and put his own rugs away. He is apt not to send his children to school when there is a festival of the Muses; he will say they are unwell, and so save their contributions. When he goes marketing, he brings the meat and green-stuff home himself under his cloak. When his cloak has gone to the fuller he stays indoors. If a friend is raising a subscription and has already spoken to him about it, when he sees him coming, he will turn out of his way and go home by a circuitous route. He will not buy a maid for his wife, although she brought him a dowry, but hires a girl from the women's market to attend upon her when she goes out. He wears shoes that are patched and cobbled, declaring that the leather is as strong as horn. As soon as he gets out of bed he will sweep the house and dust the furniture; and when he sits down he turns up the coarse cloak which is for him the only wear.

26. *The Avaricious Man*

Avarice is excess in the matter of base gain.

The avaricious man is one who when entertaining friends does not supply them with enough bread. He will borrow money from a guest who is staying with him for a night. When he is dividing food into portions, he will say it is only right that the distributor should have a double share; and straightway take it. If he is selling wine, he will water it, even though the purchaser is a friend. He only goes to the theatre when the lessees give gallery seats free; and then he takes his boys with him. When he travels abroad on a state embassy, he leaves at home the travelling-money the Treasury has paid him, and borrows from his colleagues; he gives his servant, too, more baggage than he can carry, and supplies him with less food than any of the rest; he demands, too, his full share of the ambassadors' rations—and then sells it. When he is anointing himself at the bath-house he will say to his slave: "Why, this oil you bought is rancid," and borrow from someone else. If his servants find some coppers in the street, he is apt to demand his part and will cry "Go shares." When he has sent his cloak to the fuller, he will borrow another from a friend and allow weeks to pass before he returns it, and then not until he is asked.

These are the sort of things he does. He will weigh out his household their rations with his own hand, using a short measure with a dinted bottom and carefully brushing the rim. When a friend expects the market-price for some goods, he will take advantage of him, and later on dispose of them himself at a profit. If he is paying a debt of one hundred and twenty pounds, he is very likely to be four shillings short. When his sons through illness have not been to school during the month, he will deduct in proportion from the master's fee; and in the month Anthesterion, as there is so much to see then, he does not send them to their lessons at all, and so avoids paying anything. When he is receiving rent from a slave he will demand also the discount due on payments made in copper money. At a clan dinner he will go into accounts with the secretary, asking for food for his slaves from the common stock and making a careful note of the half-radishes left over, so that the waiters may not have them. When he is travelling with acquaintances, he will make use of their slaves and let his own out on hire; but he will not put their wages into the common purse. If a joint dinner is held at his house, he is very apt to hide away some of the firewood and lentils and vinegar and salt and lamp-oil that have been provided. If a friend is marrying or getting his daughter married, he will go away just beforehand to avoid giving a present. And he will borrow from people he knows things that you would not ask for again, or be in any hurry to take if they were offered you.

27. *The Coward*

Cowardice would seem to be just a mental collapse due to fear.

The coward is one who on a sea-voyage will protest that each promontory is a privateer; and if it gets rough will ask: "Is there anyone on board who has not been initiated?" He will pop up his head and inquire of the steersman if he is half-way yet, and what he thinks of the weather; telling the person next to him that he is a little nervous because of a dream he had. He will take off his tunic and give it to his slave in case he has to swim, or he will ask to be put ashore.

Should he be serving in a land campaign he will call to a rescue-party, and bid them stand by him a moment and have a look round, remarking that it is difficult to discover which are the enemy. Hearing a noise of shouting and seeing men falling, he will say to those near him that in his haste he has forgotten his sword and will run back to his tent. Once there he sends his slave away to reconnoitre the enemies' position, and hiding his sword under his pillow, spends hours pretending to look for it. Seeing from the tent a wounded comrade being carried in, he will run up to him and bid him cheer up and take him in his arms and carry him. He will attend him and sponge him and sit beside him and keep the flies off his wound—in fact, he will do anything rather than fight the enemy. When the bugler sounds the signal for battle, he will cry, as he sits in his tent: "Go to the devil. You won't let the man get a wink of sleep with your ever-lasting trumpeting." Then, covered with blood from the other's wound, he will meet those returning from the battle and explain how at considerable risk he has saved one of his friends, and will fetch the demesmen and the members of his tribe to see the wounded man, telling each of them that with his own hands unaided he carried him to the tent.

28. *The Superstitious Man*

Superstition would appear to be purely cowardice in regard to the supernatural.

The superstitious man is one who will wash his hands very carefully, sprinkle himself from the vessel at a temple door, put a piece of laurel in his mouth, and so go about all day. If a weasel runs across his path, he will not go on until someone else has traversed the road, or he has thrown three stones over. When he sees a snake in his house, if it is a yellow one, he calls on Sabazios; and if it is of the sacred kind, he straightway sets up a shrine on the spot. He will pour oil from his flask on the smooth stones at the cross-ways as he passes by, and will kneel down and say his prayers before he resumes his journey. If a mouse nibbles through a meal-sack, off he goes to the professional religious adviser and inquires what is to be done; and if the answer is: "Give it to a cobbler and have it mended," he pays no attention, but goes away and expiates the omen by sacrifice. He is apt to be constantly purifying his house, saying that Hecate has been brought in by witchcraft. If an owl screeches as he passes, he cries out in alarm: "Save us, Athene," before he goes any further. He will not tread upon a grave, or come near a corpse or a woman in child-bed, saying that it is best for him not to incur pollution. On the fourth and twenty-fourth of each month he will order his servants to mull some wine, and going out will purchase myrtle, frankincense and cakes, and on his return will spend the rest of the day in crowning the Hermaphrodite statues. When he has had a dream, he will visit the interpreters, the soothsayers, the augurs, and ask them to what god or goddess he should pray. Every month he will repair to the priests of the Orphic mysteries to partake of the holy rites, accompanied by his wife, or, if she is busy, by his children and their wet-nurse. He would seem also to be one of those people who zealously sprinkle themselves with sea-water; and if ever he sees anyone making a meal of the garlic left for Hecate at the cross-roads, he will run away, pour water over his head, and get a priestess to carry a squill or a puppy round to purify him. And if he sees a madman or an epileptic, he will shudder and spit on to his gown.

29. *The Oligarchical Man*

The oligarchical spirit would seem to be a love of authority which covets not gain but power.

The oligarchical man is the sort of person who, when the people are considering whom they shall elect to serve with the archon on the Procession Board, will come forward and declare that the commissioners should have plenary powers; and if someone proposes there should be ten, he will say: " One is enough; but he must be a *man*." The only line of Homer he can quote is:

The rule of the many is evil; let the ruler be one;

of the rest he knows nothing. He is very apt to use these sorts of phrases: " Let us meet and discuss these matters by

ourselves, away from the crowd and the market-place";
"We must stop this running after office and submitting to
the insults or the favours of these fellows"; "Either they
or we must govern the State." He will go out at noon with
his cloak carefully adjusted, his hair fashionably cut, and his
nails neatly trimmed, and will strut along Odeon Street
making such remarks as these: "There is no living in
Athens with these informers"; "We are disgracefully
treated by the juries"; "I wonder why people want to
meddle with affairs of State"; "How thankless the mob is,
always at the mercy of a largess or a bribe!" "How ashamed
I feel when a poor dirty fellow sits down next me in the
Assembly!" "When," he will cry, "are they going to stop
ruining us with their public services and ship-equipments?"
"How hateful is the demagogic tribe! Theseus was the cause
of all this trouble. It was he who reduced us from twelve
states to one, and subverted the monarchy. But he got his
deserts; he himself was the people's first victim." And so
on, and so on, to foreigners, and to those citizens who are of
like mind and opinion with himself.

30. The Patron of Rascals

To patronise rascals shows a certain taste for vice.

The patron of rascals is one who seeks the company of
those who have been convicted of a criminal offence and
incurred a fine, thinking that if he has them for friends he
will gain experience of life and be regarded with greater
awe. Speaking of honest men he will say that no one is
naturally honest, all men are alike; and then with a sneer—
"Honesty, forsooth!" He will tell you that such and such
a rascal is merely a man without prejudices, if you look at
things rightly. "Most of the things that people say of him
are true, I allow; but there are some facts they do not take

into account: for instance, he is a witty fellow, tactful, and a staunch friend." And he will insist that he has never met a more capable fellow. He will back him up when he is speaking in the Assembly or appearing as defendant in court; and he is apt to tell the jury to consider not the person but the merits of the case. " He is the people's watch-dog "— he will declare—" and protects them from evil-doers. If we lose such men as him, we shall have no one to take the public wrongs to heart." He is fond, too, of setting up as a champion of rascals, and to form conspiracies on a jury to further a bad cause; and when he is hearing a case, he puts the worst construction on what both litigants say.

THE ALEXANDRIAN AGE

THE ALEXANDRIAN AGE

THEOCRITUS

The Women at the Festival. Idyll xv.

Gorgo, a Syracusan lady residing in Alexandria, attended by her
waiting-woman Eutychis, pays a call on her suburban friend
Praxinoë, and after some conversation takes her to the festival of
Adonis at the palace of King Ptolemy. In form, the piece is a very
skilful adaptation of the hexameter metre to the requirements of
the mime: in substance, it shows plainly how different the position
of women in Alexandrian society was from what it had been in
Athens. The translation is made from the text of Wilamowitz-
Moellendorff: the stage directions are my own.

SCENE I

*A room in Praxinoë's villa. In the centre stands a spinning-
wheel, at which the lady of the house is working: her maid
Eunoë is carding wool for her to spin: her little boy
Zopyrion is playing on the floor*

Gorgo [*entering*]. Praxinoë in?
Praxinoë [*starting up*].   Yes, indeed. Oh, my dear,
     What a pleasant surprise! So you really are here!
     [*To Eunoë.*] A chair and a cushion. Now, Gorgo, sit down.
Gorgo [*settling herself comfortably*]. That's nice. It's as well
          I've a mind of my own,
     Or else I should never have got here alive.
     What a crowd! And the cars! And the way that they
          drive!
     The soldiers in uniform look very smart;
     But the distance! We really live too far apart.
     axinoë [*beginning a favourite subject*]. That madman of
          mine is the cause of it all.

He *would* take this hovel—for no one can call
It a house—at the end of the earth, so that we
Might never a glimpse of each other's face see.
The mean jealous wretch, he loves nothing but strife,
And he's been just the same all the days of his life!
Gorgo [*pointing to the little boy*]. Don't run down your
      husband, my dear, or get wild
When the little one's here. Have a care for the child.
How frightened he's looking. [*To Zopyrion.*] Now, don't
      be afraid,
'Twas not meant for papa what your mother just said.
Praxinoë [*indifferently*]. Good lord, he takes notice.
Gorgo.   Nice pa!
Praxinoë [*with more vigour*].   Yesterday—
    Or so we will call it—to get him away
I sent him to buy me some rouge and saltpetre;
And he came back with—*salt*, the great big silly creature.
Gorgo [*warming to the topic*]. Well, mine is the same, a real
      terror with cash!
Seven shillings apiece for the merest old trash.
Five fleeces, forsooth! Nasty, dirty dog skins!
It's trouble on trouble when once he begins.
          [*Interrupting herself.*]
But come, let's be off. At the Palace to-day
It's the feast of Adonis. The queen, people say,
Does things grandly. So put on your shawl and your cloak.
Praxinoë [*spitefully*]. Fine feathers, of course, always go with
      fine folk.
Gorgo [*in a soothing voice*]. What a tale to the stay-at-homes
      you'll have to tell!
Come along.
Praxinoë [*still grumbling*]. Ah, for idlers that's very well;
They never are busy; but I've work to do.
    [*To Eunoë.*] Gather up all my wool: put it in the bureau.

Stir yourself, lazybones. You cats love to lie still,
Asleep on a cushion. I'll teach you, I will
Quick now with some water; I must have a wash.
I did not say soap! Pour it out and don't splash.
You're wetting my clothes. Oh, good lord, what a mess!
Well, that's over. Now fetch me the key of the press.
[*Goes to the clothes-press and brings out a new bodice.*]
Gorgo [*exclaiming*]. What a sweet pretty bodice! How awfully
    nice!
And what beautiful fabric! Pray, tell me the price.
Praxinoë [*gloomily*]. Don't talk of it. Eight pounds I paid
    for the stuff
As it came from the weaver's loom quite in the rough,
And the work on it brought me almost to death's door.
Gorgo [*consoling*]. Well, it is *most* successful. No one could
    wish more.
Praxinoë [*slightly mollified*]. Many thanks. [*To Eunoë.*] Now
    my shawl; and then put on my hat
In the way it should go. [*To Zopyrion.*] No, I shan't take
    you, brat.
Biting horse, big black bogey! It's no use to cry.
Would you like to have both your legs broken and die!
[*To the nurse.*] Take care of the child, Nan, and help him
    to play:
Call the dog in—and lock the door while I'm away.
    [*With these parting injunctions the two ladies,*
    each attended by her maid, at last manage to
    leave the house.]

SCENE II

The streets of Alexandria: filled with a motley throng of Greeks
and Egyptians, Syrians and Jews. The soldiers of
Ptolemy's body-guard, in their jack-boots and full cloaks,
jostle pale scholars from the Museum, who, in their turn,

rub shoulders with *flute-girls* and *respectable matrons.*
The whole crowd is moving slowly towards the Palace.
Praxinoë. Ye gods, what a throng! Shall we ever get through?
They're like ants beyond counting, this jostling crew.
But thanks to our monarch, so gracious and kind,
Rogues now don't come creeping up to you behind
In the old Egypt fashion, and try some sly game,
Like they once used to play at without any shame.
Since his father went up to high heaven to rest,
Of his many good deeds this is surely the best.

> [*These patriotic sentiments occupy the time while the
> ladies are pushing their way to the Palace. They
> have just arrived at the royal square when a troop
> of cavalry approach.*]

Praxinoë. Ah, here come the horses! Oh, what shall we do?
My good sir, be careful; don't tread on me. Oh!
Look how that bay's rearing. Get out of his way,
You foolhardy girl. [*To Eunoë.*] I am sure that this day
He'll be doing some mischief. It's lucky for me
That my brat stayed at home, or how scared I should be.
Gorgo [*taking Praxinoë's hand*]. We're safe: they've gone
past to their place on parade.
Praxinoë [*slightly recovering from her agitation*]. Of horses
and snakes I've been always afraid
Ever since my young days. Ah, I feel better now.
Quick, or we'll be swamped in this huge overflow.

> [*As they move slowly towards the Palace they meet an
> old lady coming in the opposite direction.*]

Gorgo. Have you come from the Palace?
The Old Lady.   Yes, pretty one, yes.
Praxinoë. And can we get in without too much distress?
The Old Lady. By trying the Greeks got to Troy in the end.
If you try hard enough, you'll succeed, little friend.

> [*She passes on.*]

Gorgo. The oracle's spoken—and now she has gone.

Praxinoë. Ah, women know everything, how it is done:
   Yes, even how Zeus married Hera.
                    [*By this time they have arrived at the Palace.*]

Gorgo.   Oh dear,
   There's a terrible crowd round the Palace, I fear.

Praxinoë [*taking charge of her party*]. It's wonderful. Gorgo,
        cling close to my arm:
   If we keep all together we shan't come to harm.
   You, Eunoë, hold on to Eutychis tight.
   Don't separate, then we shall get in all right.
     [*They are now in the thick of the crowd trying to pass
        through the Palace gate.*]
   Oh dear, how unlucky! My skirt's torn in two.
   Take care of my shawl, sir, whatever you do,
   And may the gods love you!

A Good-natured Man.   I'm trying my best;
   But I scarcely can help it, so closely we're pressed.

Praxinoë. What a jostling crowd, packed like pigs all around!

Good-natured Man. Don't be scared, little lady, we're quite
        safe and sound.
                [*He gives what assistance he can to the ladies.*]

Praxinoë [*fervently*]. And may you live safe, sir, for ever
        and aye!
   [*To Gorgo.*] What a nice thoughtful man, and most kind,
        I must say!
   Look at Eunoë there getting squeezed. Come along;
   You must push your own way, silly girl, in this throng.
   Now close up together.
                    [*With one final effort they enter.*]
              We're right now inside—
   As the bridegroom remarked when locked in with the bride.

Scene III

*A large hall in the Palace, arranged as a mortuary chapel,
full of people talking, gazing, and waiting for the lament
to be sung. Upon a raised daïs on a bier decked with
embroidered cloths lies an ivory statue of Adonis half-
covered with garlands of red roses.*

Gorgo [*to Praxinoë*]. Come close and look first at these
          broideries, dear.
  How lovely and light! I am sure that gods wear
  Such garments as these, they're so wonderfully fine.

Praxinoë [*standing in ecstasy before the bier*]. Who spun this
          fair fabric, who drew this design
  So true to the life, where each pictured form stands
  Like a real breathing creature, not made by man's hands!
  Athene! What clever things mortals can do!
  And look at Adonis, how beautiful too
  He seems, as he lies on his broad silver bed;
  Thrice-lovéd Adonis, beloved 'mid the dead!

An Irritable Stranger [*waiting impatiently for the music to
begin*]. You wearisome creatures, I wish you'ld go hang!
  With their endless sing-song and their broad Doric twang.

Gorgo [*indignantly*]. Ah! Where may this person come from?
          If we please,
  We shall chatter like this all the day at our ease.
  We are women of Syracuse, if you must know:
  And when we speak Doric, I think you'll allow
  That Corinthians sprung from Bellerophon's stock
  May talk the old tongue. Sirrah, rule your own flock.

Praxinoë [*joining in the fray*]. By our lady, we don't want
          more masters than one.
  We shan't come to *you*, when our rations are done.

Gorgo. Hush, dearest! The Argive is going to sing
  The dirge for Adonis, a most lovely thing.

At last year's performance this girl was confessed
Of all the dirge singers to be quite the best,
And this year I fancy she'll do better yet.
Look how she is preening herself, pretty pet!
[*The singer comes forward and begins the long ritual lamentation.*]

The Singer

Queen that dwellest on Idalium, and in Golgi dost delight,
Aphroditë, golden sporting, whom we pray on Eryx height,
They have brought Adonis to thee from the eternal stream
 below,
In the twelfth month they have brought him; for albeit their
 feet are slow,
Yet we know the Hours are kindly and some gift they ever
 bring,
And we long to speed their coming as to earth their way they
 wing,
Even as on Berenicë fell thy effluence from the sky,
Giving to her mortal body grace of immortality!

Therefore now, O many-templed Cypris, thou of many a
 name,
Queen Arsinoe, her daughter, fair as Helen, for thy fame
Cherishes thy dear Adonis with ripe fruit and gardens rare
Set in silver baskets and with incense burnt in golden ware.
All the cakes that women fashion, mingling with the wheaten
 flour
Oil and honey and sweet blossoms, here before his feet we
 pour,
Shaped as birds or creeping insects, while around his anised
 bed
Little Loves like nestlings flying try their pinions overhead.

Lo, the gold and polished ebon and the eagles ivory white
Bearing up to Zeus his minion, Ganymede, the god's delight.
Lo, the purple strewn about him, purple softer e'en than sleep
Dyed on fleeces of Miletus and the wool of Samian sheep,
So that Samos and Miletus will, alike triumphant, say—
" We it was who decked the pallet where beloved Adonis
          lay."
Here the Cyprian, there Adonis, each upon their couch
          recline;
Beardless groom, and silk soft kisses, given to the bride divine.

So to-night we leave her sleeping with her lover free from
          pain;
But, when morning's dews are falling, we shall gather here
          again,
And shall lift our dear Adonis and shall bear him to the sea,
Where the breakers foam about us, rushing from the ocean
          free.
And before we cast him from us we will loose our unbound
          hair
On our shoulders, and to heaven will our bruiséd bosoms bare,
While our kirtles fall unfastened and in lamentable throng
We bewail the lost beloved and repeat our sad sweet song.

" Thou alone, beloved Adonis, of the heroes, as men tell,
Hast the power to dwell with mortals and by Acheron to
          dwell.
Ne'er to Agamemnon was this granted, nor to Ajax wild,
Nor to Pyrrhus and Patroclus, nor to Hector, Priam's child,
Nor to Pyrrha's offspring, nor to all the Lapith chiefs of old,
Nor the princes of great Argos, nor the sons of Pelops bold;
Bless us now, beloved Adonis, bless us in the coming year!
Dear has been this advent to us, and that advent will be dear."
          [*The song ends.*]

Gorgo. She's really too clever. What wonderful skill,
And what a sweet voice! How I envy her. Still
It's time to be going; it's past dinner-hour,
And my Diocleides will look very sour
If there's nothing to eat and he's hungry. Oh dear;
Unless he's well fed he's a regular bear!
Farewell then, Adonis, at peace may you lie
And give to us peace! Dear Adonis, good-bye.

HERODAS

The Go-between. Mime i.

The *Mimes* of Herodas, realistic pictures of middle-class life put in dramatic form, were written for an Alexandrian audience about 270 B.C. In them women play the same important part as they did in the social life of the time. The translation is made from the text of Walter Headlam.

Scene: *A Room in Metrichë's House.*

Metrichë. Threissa, someone's knocking at the door. Go and see if anyone has come from our friends in the country.

Threissa. Who's there?

Gyllis. I.

Threissa. Who are you? Are you afraid to come close?

Gyllis. Here I am, quite close to you.

Threissa. But who are you?

Gyllis. Gyllis, Philainion's mother. Go in and tell Metrichë that I am here.

Metrichë [*calling*]. Ask the person to come in. Who is it?

Gyllis [*entering*]. Gyllis, old mammy Gyllis.

Metrichë. That will do, Threissa. What kindly fate induced you to come here, Gyllis, like a visitor from heaven? It's five months, I should think, since anyone has seen you— even in a dream—coming to my door; and that I swear.

Gyllis. I live a long way off, my child, and the mud in the streets comes up to my knees. Besides, I have no more strength than a fly. Old age is hard upon me and death's shadow draws near.

Metrichë. Hush, hush! Don't malign your years. You can hug a man still, I warrant.

Gyllis. Laugh away, my dear: that is a young lady's privilege.

Metrichë. You are not offended, are you?

Gyllis. Well, my child, how long are you going to stay a widow, pining away in a lonely bed? It's ten months since Mandris set off to Egypt, and never a line has he sent you. Ah! he has forgotten you now, and drinks from a new cup. Egypt is Aphroditë's true home. Everything—all that exists and all that is produced in the world—is to be found there: wealth, wrestling-schools, power, peace, glory, theatres, philosophers, money, young men, the precinct of the divine brother and sister, the best of monarchs, the museum, wine, all the good things you can desire—and *women.* Oh! the number of them! By our lady, they are more than the stars in heaven; and in beauty they are like the goddesses who went once to Paris to have their charms judged. I hope that they do not hear me! My poor dear, what sort of life is yours, warming your cold bed! You will find yourself an old woman before you know it, and your youthful bloom will turn to dust and ashes. Look somewhere else; change your way of life for two or three days; be merry, and have an eye for another man. A ship moored with one anchor is none too safe, you know. Should death come, no one can ever raise us up again. The winter storms blow furiously, and none of us knows the future. For unhappy mortals, life is an uncertain thing. My dear, is there anyone close by?

Metrichë. No, no one.

Gyllis. Then listen to the proposal which I came here to make. Gryllus, the son of Matakinë, Pataikio's wife, has won five prizes at the games: once as a boy at Pytho, twice at Corinth among the beardless youths, and twice at Pisa in the men's boxing. He is very wealthy also; so gentle that he would hardly break a twig; and in matters of love an intact seal. He saw you at the Descent of Misë,

and since then he has been all on fire and mad with longing: he never leaves my house night or day, but weeps
over me and calls me "little mother," and is near to
death's door. Now, Metrichë, my child, grant to Aphroditë
this one weakness: submit yourself to her will, lest old
age look upon you before you think. You will gain in
two ways: you will live a life of pleasure, and he will give
you more money than you can imagine. Think of it and
consent: I am only doing this for love of you, I swear it.

Metrichë. Your white hair dulls your wits, Gyllis. By
Mandris' return, and by our lady Demeter, I would not
have taken this from any other woman. I would have
taught her to sing her limping song to a limping tune, and
after to-day she would have hated my very door-step. As
for you, my dear, never come to my house again with a
proposal like this. Tell your old-wives' tales to girls, but
permit Metrichë, daughter of Pytheas, " to keep her cold
couch warm ": no one shall mock at Mandris because of
me. But Gyllis wants no sermons, I know. Here, Threissa,
wipe that cup and pour out three measures of neat wine;
just a drop of water in it will make a good drink. There,
Gyllis!

Gyllis. Pass it over, dear. I did not come here to try and
get you to go wrong. It was in a sacred cause, for
whose sake——

Metrichë. It's no good, Gyllis. Here's luck!

Gyllis. La! child. Nice stuff this, by our lady. Poor old
Gyllis has never tasted better wine than Metrichë's.
Well, good-bye, my child. Take care of yourself. I just
hope that my girls Myrtalë and Simë will stay young and
frisky so long as I have breath in my nostrils.

The Schoolmaster. Mime iii.

SCENE: *The School-room where Lampriskos is teaching. To him enter Metrotimë, dragging her son after her.*

Metrotimë. May the dear Muses, Lampriskos, give you pleasure and all joy in life, if only you will hoist this rascal and flog him till there's no more breath in his body —curse him. He has taken the roof from over my poor head with his pitch-and-toss, and he gets worse every day; knucklebones are not enough for him now. It would take him all his time to tell you where his writing-master lives —and yet his fees have to be paid, plague on it, at the end of every month—but he knows all about the gambling-den, where the porters and runaway slaves congregate, and can direct other people to it. His wretched writing-tablet, which each month I laboriously cover with wax, lies neglected by the bed-post nearest the wall. He just scowls like hell at it, and never writes anything properly, but scrapes the wax off clean. But the knucklebones in his bag are a lot glossier than our oil-flask which we use every day. He does not even recognise the sound of A, unless you yell it at him half-a-dozen times. The day before yesterday, when his father dictated *Maron*, this genius made it *Simon*, until I began to call myself a fool for not setting him to feed asses rather than to learn his letters, in the hope that I might have a support in my old age. If I or his father tell him to recite a piece, as a boy should be able to do—of course the old man is hard of sight and hearing—then out it comes, drop by drop, as though through a sieve, "Apollo-god-of-hunting." "Why, your grandmother can say that, you wretch," I shout, "although she can't read a word: and so can the first Phrygian slave you meet." If we raise our voices to reprove him, either he refuses to visit our threshold for three days, and lives off his grandmamma, poor old soul, or else he sits straddle on our roof-top, peering down like a monkey. Think what my poor heart suffers when I see him. I don't trouble so much about *him*, but the tiles are getting like broken biscuits, and when winter comes, I shall have to pay threepence each for new ones. The whole tenement cries out: " Metrotimë's boy Kottalos is responsible for this "—and it's quite true, so that soon we shall have nothing to eat. See, too, how his nose is all skinning after his woodland roamings — you would think he was a poor fisherman of Delos dragging out a weary existence at sea. But he knows the seventh and the twentieth better than the astronomers, and can't get to sleep for thinking when it will be holiday-time. Now, Lampriskos, if you want the Muses to grant you happiness and prosperity, don't give him less than——

Lampriskos. Metrotimë, you need not curse him: he will get all that he deserves in any case. Here, Euthies, Kokkalos, Phillos; quick, get him on your shoulders and let the full moon see him—it has come at last as Akeses said. Pretty goings on, Master Kottalos! You're not content to play knucklebones with your school-friends; you must needs haunt the gambling-den and play dice with the touts there. I'll make you as quiet as a girl, my lad, if that's how you behave: you won't be able to stir a twig. Hand me my stinging-whip, the bull's tail, with which I leather my gaol-birds, who won't do what they are told. Give it me before I choke with anger.

Kottalos. Nay, nay, I beseech you, sir, by the Muses, and by your beard, and by your poor little Kotty's life, don't flog me with the stinger: take another one, please.

Lampriskos. You're a bad boy, Kottalos. No one could say

a good word for you, even if he wanted to sell you in the country where mice eat iron.

Kottalos. How—how many lashes are you going to lay on, sir?

Lampriskos. Don't ask me. Ask your mother here.

Kottalos. Mamma, how many are you going to give me?

Metrotimë. By my life, as many as your miserable hide will stand.

Kottalos. Stop! That's enough, sir.

Lampriskos. Stop being a bad boy, then.

Kottalos. I'll never, never do it again. I swear it by the dear Muses.

Lampriskos. What a long tongue you have got, you rascal. I'll put the gag on you, if you say another word.

Kottalos. There, I am silent. Don't kill me, please.

Lampriskos. Let him down, Kokkalos.

Metrotimë. You should not have stopped flogging, Lampriskos, till sunset. He is more cunning than a water-snake; and even if he is at his book you should give him——

Kottalos. Nothing.

Metrotimë. Yes, another twenty at least; even if he is going to read better than the muse of history herself.

Lampriskos. Fie, madam. A little honey on your tongue would do no harm.

Metrotimë. I think, after all, I will tell the old man about this when I get home; and I'll bring some foot-straps back with me, so that as he dances here with his feet together, the Lady Muses, whom he so detests, may witness his disgrace.

OXYRHYNCHUS PAPYRI

Vol. i. page 185.

In the fifteen volumes of Egyptian papyri published by Grenfell and Hunt, 1898–1922, there is a mass of material relating to .ocial life and customs. One document alone can be here given.

A Schoolboy's Letter

Theon to his father Theon, greeting. It was a fine thing not to take me with you to town! If you won't take me with you to Alexandria, I won't write to you or speak to you or say good-bye to you. If you go to Alexandria, I won't ever take your hand nor greet you again. That is what will happen if you won't take me. Mother said to Archelaus: " It quite upsets him to be left behind." It was good of you to send me a present the day you sailed. Send me a lyre, now, I beg you. If you don't, I won't eat, I won't drink. That's that.

GREECE UNDER THE ROMANS

GREECE UNDER THE ROMANS

DION

An Euboean Idyll

Dion of Prusa, who lived in the reign of the Emperor Trajan, travelled all over the Greek-speaking world and was as well acquainted with social conditions as any man of his time. This tale, which he tells in his own person, shows us both the depopulated condition into which Greece had fallen, and also how the forms of city government were kept up while the country itself was in a state of hopeless decline.

I HAPPENED to cross the sea from Chios with some fishermen in quite a small boat, after the summer season was over. A violent storm came on, and it was with difficulty that we reached the Hollows of Euboea alive. My companions ran their craft on to the rugged shore beneath the cliffs and let it break up, while they themselves made their way to some shell-fishers, who were lying up under the neighbouring breakwater, and decided to stay there and join forces with them. I was left to myself, and not knowing to what city I should go for shelter, wandered aimlessly along the shore, hoping to find some coasting-vessel or party taking shelter from the storm. I had gone a good way without seeing a human being, when I suddenly came upon a stag which had fallen over the cliff on to the beach, and still panting was being buffeted to and fro by the waves. A little afterwards I fancied I heard the barking of dogs above my head, but the sound came faintly because of the noise of the sea.

So I went on, and climbing with great difficulty to higher ground, saw the dogs running about at a loss, whereby I inferred that the stag, being hard pressed, had leapt over the cliff. Soon afterwards I saw a man, a hunter by his looks and dress, with healthy cheeks and a generous shock of hair at the back of his head, worn in the same fashion as Homer describes with the Euboeans at Troy, making fun and mock of them because, while the other Achaeans had a full head of hair, they only allowed half theirs to grow. " Pray, stranger," he asked, " have you noticed a stag anywhere about here trying to escape? " " Yes," I replied, " there he is in the waves." And then I took him to the place and showed him. So he dragged the creature out of the water, and flayed its skin with his hunting-knife, I helping him to the best of my ability, and then cut off the hind-quarters, which he carried away, together with the skin, inviting me to come with him and partake of the meat. " My house is not far away," he said, " and to-morrow morning, after a night's rest with us, you can come down here again, for the sea now is impossible. Indeed, although I do not want to frighten you, I myself should be well content if this wind abated in five days: and that is not very likely, when our hills are as heavy with clouds as you see them now." Thereupon he asked me where I had come from, and how I had got there, and whether my boat had not been wrecked. " It was quite a small craft," I replied. " Some fishermen were making the passage, and as I had pressing business, I joined them and was the only passenger. It ran ashore anyhow and broke up." " That was only to be expected," he said. " You can see for yourself how rough and wild the sea-side of our island is. These parts are called ' The Hollows of Euboea,' and if a ship comes this way, it has no chance. Even the crew seldom escape, unless they are sailing light, as you were. But come with me and do not be afraid. For the moment, you need refreshment after your hardships; to-morrow, when we have made your acquaintance, we will do our best to arrange for your safe departure. It seems to me that you are one of those city-folk, not a sailor or workman, and you are so thin that you cannot be at all strong, I imagine."

I was only too glad to go with him; for I had no fear of treachery, possessing nothing save one poor cloak. Often before in similar circumstances during my long wanderings I had found by experience, as I found then, that poverty is the surest of shelters and protects a man against violence far more effectually than does a herald's privilege. So I followed him without alarm, the distance to his place being about five miles.

As we walked along, he told me on the way about his affairs and the manner of life he led with his wife and children. " There are two of us, my friend," he said, " and we live close together. Our wives are sisters and we both have a family of sons and daughters. We live for the most part by hunting, although we cultivate also a small piece of land. The place does not belong to us; we do not own it, nor did our fathers. They were freemen, but they were as poor as we are, herdsmen working for hire, tending the cattle of one of the rich landowners of the island, who possessed many herds both of horses and cattle, and many flocks of sheep, and many fine farms also, and much property of every kind as well as all the hills that you see. Their master, however, was put to death and all his estate confiscated— people say that it was because of his money that the Emperor had him killed—and then all the cattle were driven off to the slaughter-house, and with them some poor beasts of our own, for which no one ever paid us a penny."

(The hunter then explains to Dion how his father and his comrade, having no other means of existence, settled down in the deserted pastures with such few cattle as were left, and there maintained themselves by grazing and hunting. The two families intermarried and, although the elder men were now dead, the sons still followed their fathers' mode of life.)

R

One of us, although he is now fifty, has never yet been to town. I have only been there twice, once when I was a lad with my father, in the days when we had the herd of cattle. Some years after that, a fellow came here one morning demanding money, as though forsooth we had any, and bade me follow him to the city. We have no money, and to that I took my oath, declaring that if we had we would have given it to him at once. We entertained him as well as we could, and gave him two deer-skins; and I went back to town with him, for he said there was no help for it, but that one of us two should come and explain our position.

There I saw, as I had seen before, a number of large houses, and a strong wall outside, and some high square buildings on the wall, and a host of ships lying quietly at anchor, as though in a lake. There is nothing of the sort on the coast where you landed: that is why ships are always being wrecked. I saw all this, as well as a huge close-packed crowd, making such a terrible noise and din that I thought they were all fighting, one against the other. My man took me to some magistrate-folk, and said with a laugh: "This is the fellow you sent me to fetch. He has got nothing except his long hair and a shanty made of very stout timbers."

Thereupon the magistrates set off for the theatre, and I with them. The theatre is like a hollow gully, except that it does not extend far on either side, but forms a half-circle, and it is not made by Nature, but built of stone. You are laughing at me, perhaps, because I am trying to describe something to you with which you are well acquainted.

(The hunter then tells a long story. He was brought before the Assembly and accused by a fierce demagogue of occupying rich common-land without paying rent or taxes, and, moreover, of pursuing the trade of wrecker. Another more reasonable speaker, however, argues that to cultivate land under any conditions deserves praise, seeing that two-thirds of the country is left to neglect through lack of population; and, finally, the hunter is called upon to state his case. He tells the people the truth; that he has no money, and gains nothing but a bare subsistence; and, so far from luring ships on to the rocks by false signals, he has always helped ship-wrecked sailors to the best of his ability.)

While I was saying this, a man got up in the middle of the Assembly. " Here is another fellow," thought I to myself, " of the same sort, I suppose, going to tell lies about me." But what he said was this: " Gentlemen, for some time I have half-recognised our friend here, although I felt doubtful. I am sure of him now, and I think it would be unfair, nay even impious, not to tell you what I know of him, and so repay him in words the very great service that he rendered me in deeds. I am a citizen of this town, as you know; and so is my neighbour "—with that he pointed to the man at his side, who also rose to his feet—" and two years ago, as it happened, we both made a voyage in Socles' ship. Our craft was wrecked off Cape Caphereus, and only a few of our number got to shore. Some, who had money in their purses, were taken in by shell-gatherers. But we, who were stripped quite bare, had to plod our way up the cliff path, hoping to find shelter in some shepherd's hut, and running a good chance of dying from hunger and thirst. At last, after a struggle, we came to some shanties, and standing still shouted for help. Our friend here came out at our cries, and led us indoors, and gradually got a fire to burn, although it was not a very large one. Then he himself rubbed one of us down, while his wife did the same for the other, using fat instead of oil, which they did not possess. Finally, when the water was warm, they poured it over us to revive us after the cold. Our bath over, they gave us what clothes they had, and setting us down to table, served us with wheaten bread, while they themselves ate boiled pulse. We, too, had wine to drink, although they were content with water, and with the wine, venison in abundance, both roast and boiled. When we wanted to go away the next morning, they insisted on keeping us for three days, and then escorted us down to the level country; and at our final departure we were presented, each of us, with a piece of meat and a very fine skin. As for myself, seeing that I was still weak from exposure, our host took away his daughter's tunic and gave it to me, the girl herself putting on some other piece of stuff. That, however, I returned when we got to the village. So, gentlemen, it was to our friend here, after heaven, that we owed our lives."

(As a result of this testimonial the hunter was allowed to leave the city unpunished, and lived for the future undisturbed by politicians.)

He had almost finished his tale when we arrived at his shanty. "There was one thing," said I with a smile, "that you hid from the townsfolk, although it is your finest possession." "What is that?" said he. "This fine garden," I replied, " with all its vegetables and fruit-trees." "Ah," he said, " the garden did not exist then; we have made it later."

With that we went in and spent the rest of the day in festivity, reclining on a high couch piled with leaves and covered with skins, while the good-wife sat by her husband's side A marriageable daughter served us with food and filled our cups with a sweet dark wine. As for the other children, who shared the meal with us, they got their own food and helped themselves; so that I envied the little family their happiness, and thought their way of life the best I had ever known. I have been acquainted with the houses and the tables of the rich—private folks, satraps, and even kings— and in the past I have always thought them miserable. But they seemed more wretched then than ever, when I had my friends' poverty and freedom before my eyes, and saw that they lacked nothing of the pleasures of the table, but even here had an advantage over the great.

We had just about had enough when my host's partner

came in, followed by his son, a gentlemanly lad, carrying a hare. He blushed on entering the room, and while his father was greeting us, he himself kissed the maiden and handed the hare to her. Thereupon she gave up serving at table and sat down by her mother's side, the youth taking her place. " Is this the young lady," I asked my host, " whose tunic you took off to give to the shipwrecked mariner?" " No, no," he answered with a smile: " she has been married a long time, and has big children of her own now: her husband is a rich man in the village." " They supply you, I suppose," said I, " with all that you need." " *We* do not need anything," put in the good-wife. " *They* receive from us a share of any game we catch, as well as fruit and vegetables; for they do not possess a garden. Last year, certainly, we had some wheat from them, just for sowing, but we repaid them as soon as the harvest was in." "Are you thinking of giving this young lady also to a rich man," said I, " so that you may borrow wheat from her as well? " At that both the girl and the lad blushed, and the father replied, with a merry glance at the stripling, " No, her husband will be a poor man, a hunter like ourselves."

(Dion suggests that the young couple shall be wedded at once, and the tale ends with an account of the preparations for the marriage.)

FINIS

INDEX